The Heart of a Leader

*Saint Paul as Mentor,
Model, and Encourager*

Edward S. Little

About the cover: The painting, *The Apostle Paul*, is by artist Dustin Parent. A New Orleans native, Parent lives and works in Frenchtown, New Jersey. This painting is a part of a series called "Re-Imagining the Bible." Learn more at theartofdustin.com.

Forward
Movement
inspire disciples. empower evangelists.

The Heart of a Leader

*Saint Paul as Mentor,
Model, and Encourager*

Edward S. Little

Forward Movement
Cincinnati, Ohio

TABLE OF CONTENTS

Famous Last Words

"Et tu, Bruté? Then fall Caesar." Painful last words, these. Shakespeare's Caesar looks into the face of his killers, recognizes his beloved but unfaithful friend, gasps a word of accusation, and dies.

Charles Foster Kane, the towering figure in Orson Welles' *Citizen Kane*, speaks a mysterious last word: "Rosebud."

Thomas More, awaiting the ax, says, "I die the King's good servant, but God's first," and then turns to his executioner: "Be not afraid to do thine office."

Saint Stephen, protomartyr of the Christian faith, prays for himself and his killers. "Lord Jesus, receive my spirit...Lord, do not hold this sin against them" (Acts 7:59-60).

Aware that his death would provoke war among his successors, and asked who should inherit his conquests, Alexander the Great declares, "To the strongest!"

W. C. Fields, on the other hand, utters more prosaic final words. To a lynch mob in *My Little Chickadee*, he says, "I'd like to see Paris before I die...Philadelphia will do."

For centuries, Christians have pondered the last words of Jesus. "Father, forgive them, for they do not know what they are doing" (Luke 23:34). "Truly I tell you, today you will be with me in

Paradise" (Luke 23:43). "Woman, here is your son....Here is your mother" (John 19:26-27). "My God, my God, why have you forsaken me?" (Matthew 27:46). "I am thirsty" (John 19:28). "It is finished" (John 19:30). "Father, into your hands I commend my spirit" (Luke 23:46). On Good Friday, we mine these words for meaning. What do they tell us about Jesus? About the Father's plan to reconcile the world to himself through Jesus' death on the cross? About the depth of his love and the suffering that he is willing to endure for our sake? These questions are answered throughout the biblical narrative, and yet there is something profoundly important about the words on Jesus' lips as the nails pierce his hands and his feet. We listen to the last words of Jesus more intently. They touch our hearts as well as our minds. Last words demand our attention in a way that no others do.

Decades ago, while serving as assistant rector of St. Michael's Church in Anaheim, California, I visited an elderly parishioner named Francine in the hospital. Francine was one of those pillars who hold a community together through prayer, love, and sheer determination. Over the years, I'd come to know and respect her. When I entered her hospital room, she was asleep. I spoke her name several times and touched her hand, but she didn't respond. So I stood there for a few minutes in silence and finally said a prayer aloud. All the while, Francine slept; or so it seemed. As I turned to leave the room, she began to pray, though her eyes remained closed. Her words were clear: to this day, I can hear them in my memory. "Lord, watch over Father Ed, keep him safe, bless his ministry." And with that, her breathing became steadier, her sleep deeper. I wrote a note to her family on a business card, left it on the bedside table, and departed. Francine died that night. Did she know I was there? Or had the Lord in some miraculous way spoken through her? I'll never know. But this is certain: her last words were a blessing uttered on behalf of an inexperienced young priest. I have carried those words in my heart ever since.

We have no "famous last words" from the Apostle Paul. Ancient Christian tradition maintains that he was executed—beheaded—in 68 CE, during the persecution initiated by the Roman emperor Nero. No one, however, recorded his final words. We do not know if, like Thomas More, Paul had the opportunity to speak before the ax fell. He died off-screen, his death caught up in the social and political chaos of the era. Years earlier, long before his Christian conversion, Paul had participated in the judicial killing of Stephen (Acts 7:58; 8:1). In that grim moment, he heard Stephen pray for his executioners. Did Paul, awaiting the ax, do the same and pray for Nero? Did he, like Stephen, commend himself into Jesus' gracious care? Or did he follow the example of Isaiah's suffering servant, who "did not open his mouth" in the face of death (Isaiah 53:7)? We will never know.

The New Testament document known as the Second Letter of Paul to Timothy does not contain the apostle's last words in any literal sense. But it comes close. The letter is presented in the New Testament almost as a last will and testament—not his final spoken words, certainly, but the last piece of writing that bears his name. Paul is in prison, presumably in Rome, his execution a certainty. Few friends are with him. Alone in a prison cell, he writes to his young apprentice and traveling companion, Timothy. This, Paul tells him, is what I want you to remember. These are the essential elements of Christian ministry. Here are the tools you will need when you take on the mantle of apostolic leadership.

Most of Paul's letters appear to have been dictated. At one point, a scribe surfaces to give his own greeting (Romans 16:22). At another, Paul inserts a sentence in his own oversized handwriting (Galatians 6:11). None of this is a surprise. His letters, after all, have a kind of breathless tone. Sentences tumble out and sometimes run together. He interrupts himself and changes direction. One can imagine Paul pacing and dictating, the words fast-paced and relentless. 2 Timothy and the other pastoral epistles (more about that phrase below) seem more structured. There's nothing spur-of-the-moment about them. In these documents, Paul is carefully laying out a pastoral plan, preparing for the next season in the church's life, bringing a spontaneous community into a semblance of order.

At this point, an honest disclaimer is important. I am treating 2 Timothy as Paul's final written words, but not all biblical scholars agree that he wrote them. Three letters in the New Testament are often called the pastoral epistles because they all, in one way or another, address the need for the young church to organize itself and provide for a well-ordered Christian ministry. Two of these letters—1 Timothy and Titus—specifically name church officers: bishops (1 Timothy 3:1-7), deacons (1 Timothy 3:8-13), and elders (or presbyters, Titus 1:5-9; note that elder and bishop seem to be used interchangeably). It is true that one of Paul's indisputably genuine letters, Philippians, also mentions bishops and deacons (1:1). But in the pastoral epistles, a more systematic administrative structure is clearly beginning to develop. That, in fact, is one of the reasons why some scholars believe that the pastoral epistles were written long after Paul's death. These letters address concerns, they argue, that would not arise for decades.

Scholars cite two other reasons for rejecting Paul's authorship of the pastoral epistles: content and style. The letters, to begin with, do not contain the great themes that we find in Romans, 1 and 2 Corinthians, Galatians, or Philippians. There is nothing about salvation by grace through faith; no reference to the transforming power of the Holy Spirit; no struggle over the relationship between faith and works. These letters deal with matters foreign to the concerns that Paul typically addresses. In addition, many scholars argue, the pastoral epistles simply do not sound like Paul. The tone is more formal, the sentences more carefully crafted. It is hard to imagine the emotional author of Galatians writing (not dictating!) these systematic treatises on church organization.

Nonetheless, I believe that Paul wrote 2 Timothy and the other pastoral epistles. Why? First of all, the difference in content is natural enough. The pastoral epistles are addressed to individuals rather than church communities, and they are in effect training manuals. They presuppose, for instance, the careful doctrinal matters found in Romans but do not repeat them. Rather, they have a specific purpose: to prepare the next generation of leaders for the next season in the church's life. This is natural enough. For example, many years ago, I wrote an acolyte manual as part of a training program for liturgical assistants. Its content was entirely practical: how to carry the cross, how to light candles, how to assist the priest in preparing the altar, how to avoid dropping a cruet. There was nothing theological about this document. But the same person who wrote the acolyte manual also wrote sermons—which were, indeed, theological. Different needs call for different kinds of content. That principle was as true for the first Christians as it is for us.

Nor does the difference in style trouble me. We should not expect Paul to write the same way in every situation: Writers quite naturally tailor their style to the context of the document. Every October for sixteen years, for instance, I was required to deliver a bishop's address to diocesan convention. It is necessarily a long and formal document. The style and tone of those addresses, with carefully crafted sentences, points and sub-points and sub-sub-points, is light years removed from my typical speaking style, which tends to be informal and anecdotal. It is equally far removed from the hundreds of emails that I found myself writing every month, responding to requests for appointments and questions about church policy. Sometimes emails and text messages contained mere sentence fragments, a grammarian's nightmare. Yet those fragments came from the same keyboard that produced the bishop's address. All of us write and speak in different ways in different settings.

And so I am untroubled by the unique content and style of the pastoral epistles. I realize, however, that many of my readers may well be convinced that someone other than Paul wrote these documents. If that is the case for you, as you read this book, you can simply make a substitution. Whenever I write "Paul," you can substitute "the author of 2 Timothy." It is not, after all, the authorship that's important but rather the fact that 2 Timothy—like the other pastoral epistles and indeed other New Testament documents whose authorship is in dispute—has found its way into the canon. The church discerned something authoritative in this letter and now treats them as an essential part of the deposit of faith. Whoever wrote 2 Timothy, we read the letter as advice from a seasoned apostle to his young and probably frightened apprentice. 2 Timothy can instruct us as surely as it taught its first readers. We are all Timothy. We stand in need of mentoring. We are all Paul, with apprentices in our care.

Timothy frequently appears in the New Testament, both in the Book of Acts and in Paul's letters. We hear about him first in the midst of Paul's second missionary journey. Paul is revisiting Lystra and Derbe, two cities in what today we would call central Turkey. Paul had visited these communities during his first journey, and, almost comically, the inhabitants had attempted to worship Paul and his former companion, Barnabas, as Greek gods (Acts 14:8-18). Now, on a return trip with a new traveling companion, Silas, we meet Timothy:

> Paul went on also to Derbe and to Lystra, where there was a disciple named Timothy, the son of a Jewish woman who was a believer; but his father was a Greek. He was well spoken of by the believers in Lystra and Iconium. Paul wanted Timothy to accompany him; and he took him and had him circumcised because of the Jews who were in those places, for they all knew that his father was a Greek (Acts 16:1-3).

The controversy about Christian observance of the Torah generally, and circumcision specifically, is beyond the scope of this book. It is sufficient to say that the church in Paul's day is bicultural. Some Christians—those of Jewish origin—continue to live in accordance with the ceremonial requirements of the Law, while other Christians—those of Gentile origin—are bound to a bare minimum. (See Acts 15 for a fuller treatment of this complex issue.) When Paul recruits Timothy as a traveling companion, Paul makes a tactical decision. While there is no requirement that Timothy undergo circumcision, Timothy's mixed parentage might become known and stir needless controversy. And so, to avoid offending Jewish Christians, Timothy is circumcised.

Timothy receives occasional mention in the Book of Acts in his role as Paul's companion. When Paul travels from Beroea to Athens, for example, Timothy and Silas stay behind, rejoining Paul in Corinth (17:15; 18:5). Later, Timothy accompanies Paul on his final journey to Jerusalem (20:4). We can assume that Timothy is part of Paul's regular retinue of travelers. Frequently Luke, the author of Acts, talks about Paul and his companions in the second person plural, "we." It is likely that Timothy is included in this plural reference. That inference is reinforced by Paul's frequent references to Timothy in his letters. The letters make it clear that Paul and Timothy enjoy a close relationship as mentor and apprentice and that Paul places enormous trust in Timothy as a personal emissary.

"I sent you Timothy," Paul tells the Corinthian Christians in the midst of multi-faceted conflict, "who is my beloved and faithful child in the Lord, to remind you of my ways in Christ Jesus, as I teach them everywhere in every church" (1 Corinthians 4:17). He emphasizes this later in the same letter: "If Timothy comes, see that he has nothing to fear among you, for he is doing the work of the Lord just as I am; therefore let no one despise him" (16:10-11). Paul tells the Corinthian Christians that he and Timothy preach the same gospel: Jesus as the yes to all of God's promises (2 Corinthians

1:19). Timothy is mentioned as a companion of Paul in the opening greeting in Paul's letter to the Philippians, and in both letters to the Thessalonians. Once more, to the Thessalonian Christians, Paul dispatches Timothy as his emissary, in this case to dispute false teaching about the second coming of Jesus (1 Thessalonians 3:1-6). The letters alone make it clear that Paul invests time, energy, and heart into his apprentice.

While Paul's first letter to Timothy is not featured in this book, it does give us some important information about Paul's young understudy. I call him young because Timothy's youth was apparently an issue as the church began to anticipate a post-Paul era. "Let no one despise your youth, but set the believers an example in speech and conduct, in love, in faith, in purity. . .No longer drink only water, but take a little wine for the sake of your stomach and your frequent ailments" (1 Timothy 4:12; 5:23).

Many in the Christian community are worried about Timothy. Despite his years accompanying Paul, he seems immature, inexperienced, insufficiently prepared to lead the church. Nowadays, we might say that he lacks "gravitas." I can understand that concern. In a photo album, well hidden from public view, I've preserved a picture of myself taken around the time of my ordination to the priesthood in 1971—sporting an enormous head of hair that covered my ears, sideburns sticking out from under the hair, and huge and gawky horned-rimmed glasses. I look about twelve years old. Could anyone have taken me seriously? Paul tells Timothy that the antidote to this misperception lies in his own conduct. Set an example, he tells Timothy, and people will make their decision about you on the basis of what they see. While it's not clear if this is a public issue, Timothy also has health problems. The nature of those problems is vague, and Paul's prescribed cure sounds counter-intuitive. Wouldn't alcohol irritate his stomach? Whatever is wrong, and whatever the appropriate course of treatment, Timothy is both young and sickly. He needs bucking up. He needs a mentor to help him overcome obstacles to effective ministry. He needs someone not simply to affirm him but to direct him.

And that leads us to the unique relationship between Paul and Timothy, mentor and apprentice, outlined so vividly in 2 Timothy. How does Paul mentor Timothy? What kind of advice does he give? What concerns dominate this last written communication from the apostle, his "famous last words"? Taking this a step further, do the topics that Paul addresses in 2 Timothy touch our lives as well? I believe that they do. As we work our way through this letter, we will find time after time that Paul the Mentor is mentoring us. We are, to be sure, far removed from the first century. We live in a radically different culture. We speak a different language—not merely our spoken language but the language of our hearts. Our technology would be unimaginable to Paul. And yet, despite these differences, we find ourselves dealing with issues as indigenous to the twenty-first century as they were to the first. Like our first-century Christian forebears, we struggle with hard spiritual questions. We puzzle our way through intractable conflict. We face a world sometimes indifferent, sometimes hostile to the gospel. Like them, we wonder: What is essential—indeed, nonnegotiable—to our Christian faith, and what is peripheral? Paul the mentor has much to teach us.

There's more to the equation. Sometimes we find ourselves in the role of mentor. This may be an official designation. For example, on three occasions, I was given the assignment of coaching recently ordained bishops, walking alongside them in the early years of a new and frequently stressful ministry. More often, however, we mentor people informally: students, co-workers, members of a sports team, neighbors, and of course, our children. What does it mean to be a model, teacher, mentor, and coach? Do we impart knowledge? Or is mentoring more than simply information-sharing? I'm convinced that mentoring is as much about personal qualities as it is about teaching protocols, processes, and data. We mentor others by showing them how to live, not simply by giving them guidelines and helpful tips.

We are, all of us, temporary fixtures. Every bishop, for instance, is given a number. I'm the seventh bishop of Northern Indiana. There is now an eighth, and at some point, he will be succeeded by the ninth. We do our bit and move on, passing the baton—or in my case, the crozier—to the next generation. That phenomenon is true not simply for the small percentage of the Christian community who are ordained (they represent only about .05 percent of the church) but for every Christian. We are all here for a short time. Jesus summons us, sets his seal upon us, works through us, and calls us home. The roles of mentor and apprentice, leader and protégé, teacher and student are not optional in the kingdom of God. They are at the heart of what it means to be a disciple of Jesus Christ. The word disciple means "one who is taught." On occasion, we find ourselves on the teaching side of the mentor/apprentice relationship; at other times, we are the learners. The purpose of this book is to help us to discover more deeply what that looks like. The apostle Paul is our teacher, guide, and mentor. Timothy is our fellow student. As we serve as both teacher and student, mentor and mentee, we seek to strengthen our ministries through authentic witness and committed—zealous, even—discipleship. We know intuitively about the importance of the heart of the leader, and indeed, research backs up this claim. Transformation in our congregations, with fellow parishioners, and in our beloved wider church requires strong leaders who have clarity of belief, dedication to spiritual practice, and commitment to service to the world.

Hundreds of years after Paul wrote his final letter of advice to Timothy, Benedict of Nursia gathered a community of monks to live together as disciples of Jesus. In some ways, the monastic movement of the sixth century was a protest movement. The church, now long legal, had become lax. Christianity was fashionable. The gospel had lost its bite, its cutting edge. Some

Christians sought to re-capture the intense commitment of the early church, and did so by forming communities. Benedict was among them. During the last years of his life—he died in 545 CE—he wrote a Rule of Life for the brothers of the monastery at Monte Cassino, between Rome and Naples on the Italian peninsula. He called his community "a school for the service of the Lord."[1] The Rule, still observed today by Benedictines around the world, outlines a balanced life of work and prayer, provides guidelines for leadership, discipline, and a humility that mirrors the humility of Jesus, and reminds monks that guests are to be received like Christ.[2] Paul himself, preparing Timothy for his enormous apostolic task, might well have spoken the opening words of the Rule. As we begin our journey through 2 Timothy, Benedict's words are especially apt: "Listen, my son, to your master's precepts, and incline the ear of your heart."[3]

PART I

REMEMBER YOUR ROOTS

The TV miniseries *Roots* took the nation by storm in 1977. For eight consecutive nights, tens of millions watched the fictionalized account of Alex Haley's family. His distant ancestor, Kunta Kinte, had been stolen from his home in the Gambia, shipped inhumanely across the Atlantic Ocean in the notorious Middle Passage, and sold as a slave in Maryland. His identity taken away—his owners even re-named him Toby—Kunta Kinte struggles to remember his home, his culture, his language. In one powerful scene, Kunta carries his newborn daughter, Kizzy, into a clearing at night and lifts her high above his head, the stars shining above them: an ancient ritual of his people, a reminder of who he is and where he comes from, and an expression of hope. "Kizzy, behold the only thing greater than yourself!" Kunta Kinte cries.

When I watch this scene, I always think of Mary and Joseph in the temple, presenting their newborn son to the Lord. They meet the aged Simeon, who takes Jesus in his arms and declares, "Master, now you are dismissing your servant in peace, according to your word; for my eyes have seen your salvation." (Luke 2:29-30a). Here too is an ancient ritual (see Leviticus 12:1-8), an expression of deep rootedness in the past and of hope for the future.

Something essential is at work here. The principle applies to Kunta Kinte and Kizzy, to the Holy Family and Jesus, and to us: We can't understand who we are or what God wants from us without immersing ourselves in the past. Our hope for the future has its roots in forces often only dimly understood. It may be that the enormous success of *Roots* stemmed from an intuitive awareness that we need to come to grips with our DNA, literally and figuratively. Services like Ancestry.com point to the yearning of so many to discover where they came from. While researching one's family can become obsessive, it can also be strangely liberating. The more we learn about ourselves, the more we can present ourselves to Jesus.

At first glance, Paul's initial word to Timothy surprises us. Because 2 Timothy is, in effect, his last will and testament, one might expect Paul to plunge quickly into practical advice. Do this! Don't do that! Instead, Paul urges Timothy to take a deep breath and look backward. Remember your roots, he tells his young apprentice. Remember who you are and where you come from. Remember the people who have had an impact on your life and the experiences that have formed you as a disciple. And so, like Paul and Timothy, we will linger for a time on our roots. From what kind of family did I emerge? How did my parents' faith—or lack of it—shape my own? Who are the people whom God sent into my life as teachers, mentors, and encouragers? What events forever changed me? What were the steps that led me to Jesus, opened my heart and mind to his will and purpose, and empowered me to follow him in ways that I could never have predicted? Paul counsels Timothy to take a step back from his urgent duties and ponder his roots. We can most profitably do the same. Our apostolic calling, like Timothy's, begins with a backward glance.

Chapter One

Lois and Eunice

Paul, an apostle of Christ Jesus by the will of God, for the sake of the promise of life that is in Christ Jesus, To Timothy, my beloved child: Grace, mercy, and peace from God the Father and Christ Jesus our Lord. I am grateful to God—whom I worship with a clear conscience, as my ancestors did—when I remember you constantly in my prayers night and day. Recalling your tears, I long to see you so that I may be filled with joy. I am reminded of your sincere faith, a faith that lived first in your grandmother Lois and your mother Eunice and now, I am sure, lives in you.

—2 Timothy 1:1-5

"X," my great-grandfather wrote on the signature line of his Civil War enlistment papers. Someone else scrawled, "James Little, his mark." My great-grandfather was illiterate, but this didn't prevent him from serving in the Fifth New York Heavy Artillery regiment that, among other things, rode with General Philip Sheridan in the merciless Shenandoah Valley Campaign. The new recruit's enlistment papers include a physical description of James Little: 5 feet, 9 inches tall; blue eyes; sandy brown hair; 160 pounds. While I have no photograph of my great-grandfather, my physical description is identical to his. James Little was the source, my father told me, of our family's connection to the Episcopal Church. An immigrant from County Kerry, Ireland, his Roman Catholic commitment was sufficiently lax that a priest paid a call to his farm in Afton, New York. According to family lore, my great-grandfather threw the priest off the porch and then, to show his utter contempt, became an Anglican.

My gene pool is quintessentially American. My father's paternal line is Irish, but his mother was descended from the Puritan settlers of Massachusetts, staunch Congregationalists. Among my ancestors on that side of the family is Roger Conant, founder and first governor of Salem, whose statue stands in the center of town to this day. Happily, he died before the famous witch trials. Somewhere deep in that family line is Oliver Goldsmith, eighteenth-century author of *The Vicar of Wakefield*. On the other side of the family, my mother's people were Lithuanian Jews who emigrated to the United States in the early twentieth century from the city then known as Kovno and now called Kaunas. My maternal grandfather, Harry Herman, sang on the Yiddish stage in New York City and occasionally, in synagogues. His wife and my grandmother, Rose, was active in the Workman's Circle, an organization that promoted progressive social and economic causes as well as Yiddish culture. Relatives who remained in Kovno died in the Holocaust. Twice I have stood at Yad Vashem, the Holocaust memorial in Jerusalem, and wept as I looked at photographs from the infamous Kovno Ghetto, where tens of thousands died. These were my people.

All of us have a DNA trail, for good or for ill. Instinctively, when a baby is born, we look for family resemblances. Does she have grandma's ears or Aunt Harriet's chin? Is his nose like Cousin Fred's? Even superficial facial characteristics remind us of our roots, as do gifts, talents, strengths, and weaknesses. Why is it that temper seems to run in some families, or a tendency to addiction, or difficulty in forming stable relationships? And why do some people seem to inherit, say, gifts of writing or painting or athletic dexterity? Some of this, of course, is learned behavior; some may be embedded in our genes. Whatever the origin, the more we learn about our families, the more we understand ourselves—even if, at times, the information can be painful.

And so it was with Timothy. Paul begins this letter in typical fashion. "Paul, an apostle of Christ Jesus by the will of God, for the sake of the promise that is in Christ Jesus;" and then, naming his addressee, he mentions the deep bond that they share: "To Timothy, my beloved child." This is startling indeed. Paul regularly calls fellow Christians as "brothers and sisters," indicating a kind of filial parity. At one point, he refers to the Christians in Corinth as his spiritual children: "Indeed in Christ Jesus I became your father through the gospel" (1 Corinthians 4:15). But this is an exception, and it is Paul's way of reminding the Corinthians that he was their founding pastor. His address to Timothy, on the other hand, has a more intimate feel. As we move through this letter, it will become increasingly clear that the bond between Paul and Timothy was as profound as that between father and son. Paul had invested himself in this young man in the way that a parent does in a child. The remainder of the greeting, while there are parallels in Paul's other letters, feels uniquely personal in this context. "Grace, mercy, and peace from God the Father and Christ Jesus our Lord. I am grateful to God…when I remember you constantly in my prayers night and day. Recalling your tears, I long to see you so that I may be filled with joy."

And then Paul turns to Timothy's family of origin. "I am reminded of your sincere faith, a faith that lived first in your grandmother Lois and your mother Eunice and now, I am sure, lives in you." While the reference is brief, we can draw some important inferences. Timothy's grandmother and mother were early Pauline converts, probably turning to Christ during Paul's first missionary journey, when he passed through Lystra (Acts 14:8). By the time that Paul returned to the region, Timothy was already a Christian

(Acts 16:1-2). We do not, however, know the details. Sometime between Paul's first and second journeys, Timothy had become a disciple. The only thing we know with certainty is that Lois and Eunice were essential in Timothy's own conversion. Later on in 2 Timothy 3:15, we'll learn that their home was saturated in the Bible. It is sufficient to say at this point that Lois and Eunice passed on their faith in Jesus to their grandson and son. Did Timothy see something in them that sparked a yearning? Did Lois and Eunice pray aloud and include Timothy in their devotions? How did they teach the faith to this impressionable young man? We simply don't know.

Nor do we know the nature of Timothy's conversion. Was it sudden and dramatic like his mentor Paul's? Or in slow and imperceptible stages? Whatever Lois and Eunice did, and however they shared their Christian faith, something happened in that home that changed Timothy forever. Godly parenting and grandparenting bore fruit in a disciple who would carry on the ministry of the Apostle Paul. And so Paul begins his final instructions to Timothy by asking him to remember his forebears and the profound way that they had shaped his life.

Two disclaimers are in order. To begin with, not every Christian parent and grandparent can tell a story like Timothy's. The path to faith is far from linear and predictable. For Christians who struggle without apparent success to commend their faith to their children, the story of Monica is encouraging. A deeply committed Christian, Monica agonized over her son, Augustine, a brilliant and headstrong young man, at once scholarly and lustful. In his *Confessions*, Augustine describes the long and apparently fruitless years that Monica prayed fervently for her son. When Monica asked a bishop to intervene in her son's increasingly disordered life, the bishop had wise words for the distraught mother: " 'Leave him alone,' he said. 'Just pray to God for him. From his own reading, he will discover his mistakes and the depth of his profanity…It cannot be that the son of these tears should be lost.'"[4] Augustine moved from North Africa to Rome and then to Milan, exploring philosophies as diverse as Manichaeism and Neo-Platonism, teaching rhetoric, and living with a mistress. Meanwhile, Monica prayed. Slowly, Augustine began to change. Ever so tentatively, he explored the Christian faith, and one day, sitting in a garden with his friend Alypius, he heard the singsong voice of a child. "Take it and read, take it and read." Augustine's eyes fell upon an open New Testament and a passage from Paul's Letter to the Romans: "Not in reveling and drunkenness, not in debauchery and licentiousness, not in quarreling and jealousy. Instead, put on the Lord Jesus Christ, and make no provision for the flesh, to gratify its desires" (Romans 13:13-14). "Then we went in and told my mother—she had moved from North Africa to Milan—"who was overjoyed."[5] Monica died shortly after her son's conversion, her decades of prayer finally answered. Monica's story reminds us that Christian parents do not always see immediate results. The long view is often the preferred view.

A second disclaimer parallels the first. Timothy and his mentor could point with gratitude to Lois and Eunice, forebears in the family and in the faith. That experience, however, is far from universal, either in the Bible or in our own lives. A few years ago, on a lark, I entered the name of an ancestor in an internet search. To my surprise, his name popped up immediately—in a newspaper article dating back to the 1920s describing his arrest on a charge of stock fraud. While this ancestor had died years before my birth, I knew him by reputation. His name was always spoken with reverence at family gatherings. The truth, it turned out, was somewhat more complicated.

Jesus' family tree, outlined in Matthew 1 and Luke 3, reminds us that his gene pool was also at best "mixed." Matthew's list of forty-two ancestors includes villains as well as heroes, the fallible as well as the faithful. Even the heroes among Jesus' ancestors have a spotty record. Abraham was, indeed, "the ancestor of all who believe…the father of all of us" (Romans 4:11,16). "By faith Abraham obeyed when he was called to set out for a place that he was to receive as an inheritance; and he set out, not knowing where he was going" (Hebrews 11:8). He is a model of faith. Yet this same Abraham, terrified during a sojourn in Egypt that Pharaoh would kill him and steal his wife, pawned Sarah off as his sister—an act of almost breathtaking cowardice (Genesis 12:10-20). As we run down Matthew's list of Jesus' ancestors, unsavory characters abound: Jacob, self-serving manipulator; Judah, fathering a child through a prostitute who turned out to be his daughter-in-law; Solomon, who built the temple in Jerusalem but whose heart was far from fixed solely on the Lord; the evil king Manasseh, who "made his son pass through fire in the valley of the son of Hinnom, practiced soothsaying and augury and sorcery, and dealt with mediums and with wizards" (2 Chronicles 33:6). These are only a few of the disreputable forebears of the King of kings. Luke's version of Jesus' genealogy reminds us of the ancestor we all share: Adam, the proto-sinner (Luke 3:38). Timothy's superb spiritual lineage, while a testimony to the faithfulness of Lois and Eunice, is a happy exception to the reality with which some (or perhaps many) Christians struggle. We too have our share of disreputable forebears.

Our family roots can be a source of pain as well as joy, and pondering those roots can take us down dark and twisted roads. The psalmist has some encouraging words as we embark on this journey:

> For you yourself created my inmost parts;
>> you knit me together in my mother's womb.

> I will thank you because I am marvelously made;
>> your works are wonderful, and I know it well.

> My body was not hidden from you,
>> while I was being made in secret
>> and woven together in the depths of the earth.

Your eyes beheld my limbs, yet unfinished in the womb;
　　all of them were written in your book;
　　they were fashioned day by day,
　　when as yet there was none of them.

—Psalm 139:13-16

The psalm points us to something fundamental about our true spiritual roots. In the womb, we developed according to nature's plan, our chromosomes shaping us, physical characteristics already determined, the positive and negative in our genetic inheritance firmly planted. Even before our parents began to raise us, much had been set in place. But Psalm 139 tells us that even DNA has its limits. From the moment of our conception, when you and I were a mere collection of molecules, God knew us. In a universe so vast that our minds cannot fathom our own galaxy or the billions of galaxies beyond, the One who created it all formed us in the womb, knit us together, and made us the object of his eternal concern. It is not a question of how this happens. God's omniscience is unfathomable. We cannot understand the mechanism behind God's intimate knowledge of every human being, nor the greater mystery that God knew us even before we were conceived and called us to his service (Jeremiah 1:5). In all of this, we look at our families of origin through God's eyes.

Our experience may be as positive as Timothy's, as rebellious as Augustine's—or as mixed as my own. The son of a nominally Anglican father and a nominally Jewish mother, I was baptized as a baby but never brought back to church. My parents (for reasons that, to this day, I don't understand) sent me to a Roman Catholic parochial school for kindergarten. All I can remember from that year was the sheer terror of seeing nuns in full, pre-Vatican II garb. In fact, on the first day of kindergarten I threw up, so scary did Sister appear to me. When my family moved to a new home in Connecticut, it turned out that the local public elementary school's opening exercises included the Pledge of Allegiance, the singing of *My Country 'tis of Thee*—and the Lord's Prayer. (All of this was several years before the Supreme Court's decision banning such prayers.) So at an early age I learned the rhythms of the Our Father, though I didn't understand the content. That would come many years later. I mention these two childhood religious memories because they are the only such memories. No Lois and Eunice shared the faith with me. My spiritual inheritance was limited to the vague awareness that I had been baptized as a baby.

Some Christians can celebrate their childhood in the church and give thanks for the Christian parents who brought them up to know, love, and follow Jesus. These are memories to embrace with full hearts. Other Christians, however, carry the scars of childhood or adolescent rebellion—rejecting a Christian upbringing, walking away from the Christian community, saying no to Jesus—and only later, much later, returning to faith. Still, other Christians never knew the Lord in childhood. That was certainly my own experience, and it means that 2 Timothy 1:5 has a slightly unreal feel as I read it. In the end, however, Paul points us in the right direction. "Your sincere faith…lives in you." Timothy had the gift of godly forebears, and whatever the nature of the instruction they gave him, Lois and Eunice's efforts took root in his soul. That's a wonderful thing. That same faith, whatever brought it to birth, can live in us as well. The God who knit us together in our mother's womb has never abandoned us to our own devices, even when we were utterly unaware of his presence. "I have inscribed you on the palms of my hands," God tells the exiles in Babylon (Isaiah 49:16).

Paul's reminder to Timothy about his roots is an invitation for us to ponder the many ways, through or in spite of our families, that we have been drawn into the heart of Jesus. Our own journey may be as linear as Timothy's or more circuitous. Each of us has a unique set of twists and turns. There's no such thing as a standard road to Christian discipleship. Whatever the particulars, Jesus' call is relentless and unmistakable. "Oh, that *today* you would hearken to his voice!" (Psalm 95:7, emphasis mine). As we ponder the complex realities of our past, Paul asks us to fix our eyes on Jesus, to tune our hearts to his call, and to give thanks for his persistent summons: "Follow me" (John 21:19).

QUESTIONS FOR REFLECTION

1. What did your family teach you about God? What childhood memories do you carry that form and inform your faith today?

2. Jesus' family tree was mixed. What about yours? How has the painful side of your family of origin made an impact on your faith? What steps do you need to take to unlearn spiritually unhelpful lessons?

3. As a parent, or as the mentor of a young person, how have you shared and commended your Christian faith? What obstacles and challenges have you faced in doing so?

4. "It cannot be that the son of these tears should be lost," a bishop said to Monica. Who prayed for you when you were young? For whom do you pray?

CHAPTER TWO

Apostolic Hands

For this reason I remind you to rekindle the gift of God that is within you through the laying on of my hands; for God did not give us a spirit of cowardice, but rather a spirit of power and of love and of self-discipline.

—2 Timothy 1:6-7

"Ed, don't you want us to pray for you?" Roy asked. The question terrified me. It was the fall of 1977, and I had been serving as vicar of St. Joseph's Church in Buena Park, California, for about two years. A few months earlier, twenty parishioners—Roy among them—informed me that they would be attending a Life in the Spirit seminar in a neighboring parish. I had a vague awareness of what the seminar was all about, and what I heard troubled me. It was, people told me, something like Charismatic Renewal 101a, an introduction to the Holy Spirit and the gifts of the Spirit: wisdom, knowledge, discernment, healing, miracles, even tongues. Horrifying stuff, that! Clergy told grim tales of parishes torn apart by super spiritual charismatics who looked down their noses on anyone who didn't share their experience. What if that happened at St. Joseph's? One evening, shortly after I'd learned that parishioners would be attending the seminar, I paced in a field behind the church, praying that God would show me how to deal with this potential crisis. *Dear Lord, what am I do to? How can I prevent my beloved parish from being divided between charismatics and non-charismatics? How can I ward off chaos and division?* As I paced, three words popped into my head: *You must go.* Was this a command from God or simply my own pastoral common sense? I'll never know, but the imperative was clear: Go.

I took those words to mean that I too must attend the seminar. Why? To protect my people, of course! If the seminar preached heresy, I would be there to stand up and object. If the seminar suggested odd and divisive practices, I would raise a warning hand. And so, dutifully, I attended. To my surprise, the first few nights of the seminar offered nothing strange or unique. The topics were standard-brand Christianity: God's love; salvation; new life; receiving the gift of new life; nothing, in other words, to which I could take exception. As the seminar progressed, however, I discovered that I was hungry—hungry for a deeper encounter with Jesus, hungry for the power of the Holy Spirit, hungry for gifts that would enable me to serve Jesus more effectively. The seminar had awakened in me a yearning for something more, something deeper, in my walk with Jesus. But what would such a thing mean?

On the fifth night, the seminar took a scary turn. Participants were invited to come forward for prayer. The leaders called it the "baptism in the Holy Spirit," by which they meant something like the release of the power of the Holy Spirit who already resides within each believer.[6] When the seminar leaders issued their invitation, I froze. People around me streamed forward. I sat in my pew, frightened by the prospect that something bizarre would happen to me, that I would be transformed into a wild-eyed, out-of-control fanatic. It was then that Roy asked, "Ed, don't you want us to pray for you?" Before I could answer or object, he grabbed my arm and dragged me up to the altar rail. I knelt down and suddenly felt an enormous, almost crushing weight. The parishioners who'd been attending the seminar gathered around me, and twenty hands were laid on me. A friend named Jim prayed, but I never heard the prayer. No one had prepared me for the sheer weight of hands bearing down on my head or the excruciating pain in my neck, back, and knees. In that solemn moment, my own prayer was somewhat more prosaic: "Dear God, " I pleaded, "don't let me fall. Don't let me humiliate myself in front of all these people." After what seemed like eternity but was probably five minutes, the prayer thankfully ended. Nothing spiritual had happened, or so I thought. I had done my duty, allowed beloved friends to pray for me, and now I could get on with my life. I stood up, hugged my parishioners, and stumbled back to my pew.

And yet—here's the important point—the Holy Spirit showed up. Whatever I was feeling that evening, something objective happened. Hands touched my head, Christian friends prayed, and the dove once more descended. My subjective experience, as distracted as I was, does not overturn the gift that the Spirit imparted. Decades later, I regularly return to that moment. When the pressures of life and work overwhelm me, when ecclesial conflict threatens to suck the joy out of ministry, when the sheer busyness of the calendar drives out the fragile remnants of spiritual recollection, I remember that *something happened*. It may have been, at the time, disorienting and even disturbing. But the prayer prayed that day changed me forever. My roots, in other words, are not simply genetic. I am more than my DNA, and my life has been shaped by God's own supernatural intervention.

Paul reminds his young apprentice, too, that *something happened* through the laying on of hands, and the experience will shape him forever. Like us, Timothy is more than his genes. His grandmother and mother have, indeed, inspired and formed his faith. All of this is true, and all of this is a source of profound gratitude. But something else has formed him as well. Paul lays apostolic hands on Timothy's head, and in that moment Timothy's life is evermore transformed. Verses six and seven from the first chapter serve as a reminder: *Timothy, remember the weight of my hands on your head. When I'm gone, when you're in charge, when the church is under siege, when your brother and sister Christians attack one another, when they attack you, cling to your apostolic commission. Never forget, even for an instant, that you have been singled out and empowered to lead the church. The Holy Spirit has given you a gift that will never be withdrawn.*

Paul offers Timothy two important reminders. First, he says, "rekindle the gift." When Paul talks about rekindling, he implies that a flame is burning low. We don't know the details, of course, but we can infer that Timothy is wrestling with his apostolic call. Perhaps his enthusiasm has diminished or his sense of the Spirit's presence has become less intense. Did he struggle with apparently unanswered prayer? Did God somehow seem absent, a version of Saint John of the Cross's dark night of the soul? Whatever the case, it's natural enough for Christians to encounter not only the highs but also the lows of discipleship, not only the depth of intimacy with God but also a dreadful and sometimes painful distance from him. Jesus cries out, "My God, my God, why have you forsaken me?" (Matthew 27:46). Timothy's desolation may not be as complete as Jesus' on the cross. But something, clearly, is wrong.

Timothy's struggle is far from unique. Christians for two millennia have wondered why the flame burns low. Writing to his friend Malcolm about a mutual acquaintance's grim medical diagnosis, C. S. Lewis says, "The 'hiddenness' of God perhaps presses most painfully on those who are in another way nearest to Him."[7] This may well have been Timothy's experience. While we cannot know the details, we do have the command from Paul: Rekindle the gift of God. The word "rekindle" (Greek *anazopyreo*) in the New Revised Standard Version can also be rendered "fan into flame," as the English Standard Version puts it. The fire has not gone out entirely, but the embers are cooling and need immediate attention. Paul tells his young friend Timothy to start taking concrete steps to reconnect with his spiritual roots. Otherwise, the low-burning ember will die out entirely.

Paul is referring to a very specific moment in Timothy's life, noted also in 1 Timothy 4:14: "Do not neglect the gift that is in you, which was given to you through prophecy with the laying on of hands by the council of elders." This gesture, the laying on of hands, has its origin deep in the Old Testament. Moses commissions his successor, Joshua, through the laying on of hands (Numbers 27:18-23). It serves as a sign of blessing (Genesis 48:14). Jesus himself lays hands on children (Matthew 19:13-15) and on the sick (Mark 6:5). Later, Ananias lays his hands on the head of the newly converted Saul, a gesture that conveyed both healing and empowerment: "Brother Saul, the Lord Jesus, who appeared to you on your way here, has sent me so that you may regain your sight and be filled with the Holy Spirit" (Acts 9:17). The church in Antioch lays hands on Barnabas and Paul (formerly Saul) and commissions them for a journey that would take them to Cyprus and what is now central Turkey (Acts 13:3). The early church lays hands on new converts (Acts 8:17; 19:5-6), on the sick (Acts 28:8), and on those called to servant ministry (Acts 6:6). Dangers abound, however. "Do not be hasty in the laying on of hands" (1 Timothy 5:22, English Standard Version; "Do not ordain anyone hastily" in the New Revised Standard Version). Because something happens when hands are imposed, the gesture should never be employed casually. We're dealing, so to speak, with fire! The Holy Spirit works through human hands to accomplish God's supernatural purposes in us, and so the laying on of hands is never merely symbolic. This most ordinary of gestures can be the fount of the most extraordinary divine-human interaction.

When Paul lays hands on him, Timothy is forever changed. Not only has he been designated as Paul's successor, but also he is empowered for that ministry. In a season of flagging zeal, Paul asks Timothy to cling to that moment of empowerment, draw on its strength, and affirm the indelible mark that the Spirit had made on his soul. That counsel is most fitting for us as well.

Christians regularly, and properly, return to their spiritual roots. Martin Luther famously said, *Baptizatus sum* ("I am baptized") in the face of peril. No matter what befalls me, he declared in effect, I have been "marked as Christ's own for ever,"[8] and nothing can erase the fact that I belong to Jesus. Luther's affirmation echoes Paul's: "It is God who establishes us with you in Christ and has anointed us, by putting his seal on us and giving us his Spirit in our hearts as a first installment" (2 Corinthians 1:21-22). Many Christians, like Luther, cling to the objective reality of their baptism as they struggle with the day-to-day challenges of following Jesus. Other sacramental moments, too, serve as an external mark of an internal and assured reality. Something happened when we were confirmed, or ordained, or made our confession and received absolution. Something happened when we were anointed for healing. Something happened when we took our beloved's hand and made vows to be faithful forever. Something happens, time after time, when Jesus feeds us in the eucharist and gives us food for our journey with him. It is certainly true that our encounters with Christ are not limited to formal sacramental moments. Some Christians point to a dramatic public commitment as a turning point that would change them forever. Others recall a quieter, less emotional experience—a monastic retreat or a sudden and surprising insight from scripture or a deep sense of belonging to a particular community of Christians. Whatever the details, something happened.

This is more than simply nostalgia or an attempt somehow to recreate an earlier spiritual experience. I can still remember with surprising clarity the first time I worshiped in a Christian church following my conversion. As I crossed a boundary between my old life and the new one, something luminous happened. The hymns, the scripture readings, and even the sermon are still wondrously clear in my memory, at a distance of five decades. In my mind's eye, I can see the building, the clergy up front, the enormous pulpit, the pews filled with well-scrubbed and well-dressed worshipers (remember, this was many years ago!). Yet when I return to that church in my memory, the important task is not to recapture my feelings as a 19-year-old or relive the breathtaking experience of worship as a new Christian. Rather, it is to give thanks for the gift of the church and for Jesus' invitation to join a company of brothers and sisters in the adventure of discipleship. That is the spiritual root to which, most properly, I cling. Rekindle the gift.

Along with rekindling the gift, Paul tells Timothy to reclaim it. "God did not give us a spirit of cowardice," he reminds Timothy, "but a spirit of power and of love and of self-discipline." Reading between the lines, we can imagine that Timothy was frightened— and rightly so. Because he had been Paul's companion for many years, he knew well the dangers that come with apostolic ministry. Paul tells the Christians in Corinth:

> Five times I have received from the Jews the forty lashes minus one. Three times I was beaten with rods. Once I received a stoning. Three times I was shipwrecked; for a night and a day I was adrift at sea; on frequent journeys, in danger from rivers, in danger from bandits, danger from my own people, danger from the Gentiles, danger in the city, danger in the wilderness, danger at sea, danger from false brothers and sisters; in toil and hardship, through many a sleepless night, hungry and thirsty, often without food, cold and naked. And besides other things, I am under daily pressure because of my anxiety for all the churches.
>
> —2 Corinthians 11:24-28

I quote this passage at length to emphasize Timothy's personal knowledge of apostolic hazards. What Paul describes to the Corinthians, Timothy experienced in person. He had every reason to be frightened. Nevertheless, Paul tells him, God didn't give you a spirit of cowardice. Instead, when hands were laid upon you, the Lord gave you something infinitely precious.

God gave you, Paul says, a spirit of power. The Greek word is *dunamis* (root of the English "dynamite") and could be translated as power or strength or ability. In other words, God will empower Timothy to do whatever his apostolic commission requires. Is the reference to internecine church struggles? Or to the opposition he will encounter in a hostile culture? Or to the physical dangers of travel? Or even, more prosaically, to the task of giving the Christian movement the organizational structure it will need in a post-apostolic era? More likely, Timothy will need supernatural power to deal with all of these challenges!

Whenever I read this passage, I remember some wise words that Bishop Robert Rusack of Los Angeles gave me many years ago. I had just been appointed vicar of St. Joseph's Church in Buena Park. Ordained only four years, I was still proverbially wet behind the ears, at once full of myself and beset by insecurities. Although I had eagerly sought my first assignment as a solo priest and pastor, when the call came, I was filled with fear. And so I traveled to diocesan headquarters in Los Angeles, presented myself to the bishop, and said, "I'm frightened, Bishop. I've suddenly realized that the responsibility is all mine—pastoral care and administration and marrying and burying and baptizing and preaching and teaching and dealing with conflict..." I ran out of words and out of breath at the same time and then added, barely audibly, "I just don't think I can do it." Bishop Rusack said, "You can't do it. God can." And that was that. He was Paul to my Timothy. He reminded me that God has given us a spirit of power, and God will never fail us. While Bishop Rusack could not have known what would happen two years later, when twenty parishioners laid hands on me and prayed for my spiritual renewal, his statement set the stage. God not only can. God did.

God gave you, Paul tells Timothy, a spirit of love. While the Greek word *agape* is well known, the concept is surprisingly difficult to pin down. The word, both in its noun and verb form, emphasizes the self-giving (rather than self-serving) nature of love. "God proves his love [*agape*] for us in that while we still were sinners Christ died for us" (Romans 5:8). Even Jesus' command that we love one another (John 13:34-35) is set in the context of action: He has just washed the feet of his disciples, including Judas, and he will soon stretch out his arms upon the cross. When the New Testament uses the word *agape* or its cognates, the emphasis is on love as something that we do. We decide to act in a loving manner, even if our feelings rebel and our heart is cold. Tragically, the history of the church is littered with tales of loveless power, and no era is exempt. It is filled, as well, with stories of divinely empowered love, from Francis of Assisi and Father Damien of Molokai ministering to lepers to Mother Teresa on the streets of Calcutta comforting the dying. "God is love, and where true love is, God himself is there."[9] Whatever authority a Christian leader carries, and however spiritual power is exercised, it must be paired with love or it becomes mere clout.

And God gave you, Paul reminds Timothy, a spirit of self-discipline. The Greek word, *sophronismos*, can be translated "self-control" (Revised Standard Version) or even "of a sound mind" (King James Version). This quality, which at first glance seems almost pedestrian, is as divinely enabled as power and love. Self-discipline empowers Timothy—and us—to balance the competing demands of power and love, bringing them into a coherent whole. Love is the natural complement of power: Supernatural love must temper supernatural ability. Without love, power devolves into tyranny. Without power, on the other hand, love devolves into mere sentimentality. Christians are always in danger of becoming either bullies or doormats. Self-discipline, as Paul commends it to Timothy, helps us to avoid either extreme and provides a kind of internal regulator. Whatever our Christian call, be it lay or clerical, be it within the institutional church or well beyond it, the Spirit endows us with a kind of anointed calm that allows us to confront our fears and exercise power in love and love in power. As I write these words, I find myself thinking of a scene in the movie version of *To Kill a Mockingbird*. Atticus Finch stands calmly before a lynch mob. The mob is demanding that Atticus turn over Tom Robinson, imprisoned falsely for rape. Atticus is immovable, steady, loving yet fierce, *sophronismos* incarnate. This cinematic moment is iconic. I want to be like that. Paul's word to Timothy is that, surprisingly, we can. Or, more precisely: You can't. God can.

These two verses, with their exhortation to fan the flame and their triad of virtues, is a kind of training program for Christian leaders, a short course in spiritual basics and a reminder of our spiritual roots. My friend Hank showed me what this looks like in practice. He has an exacting job, serving as director of an inpatient adolescent mental health unit in a large metropolitan hospital. One day I noticed a pager on Hank's belt. That alone was a surprise, since a pager is, by today's standard, an ancient form of technology. "What's that for?" I asked him. He told me that he's on call at all times, day in and day out, weekends, evenings, whenever a crisis erupts on the unit. Emergencies are the bread and butter of his profession. Wherever he is—at home, on the beach, at a restaurant, or asleep on his bed—he must be available. "Can't you ever get free of the pager?" I asked. "No, never," he told me. "It goes off all the time, often several times during the night." "That sounds like a recipe for burnout," I replied. "How in heaven's name do you do it?" Hank struggled to answer my question. Finally he said, "I'm not sure how I do it. The days and the nights can be awfully long. But I pray a lot. And somehow God gets me through." You can't. God can. Paul's promise of power, love, and self-discipline bears fruit in the lives of Christian leaders today.

QUESTIONS FOR REFLECTION

1. Can you think of a time in your life when you experienced the Holy Spirit in a dramatic way? How did you become aware that something profound had happened? What was the effect?

2. In what ways do you need the Spirit to "rekindle the gift of God that is within you"? What are the signs that the flame is burning low? And what steps can you take to fan the flame?

3. What "apostolic hazards" do you face in your daily life? How do you respond to them?

4. How do you experience the triad of power, love, and self-discipline as you strive to follow Jesus in the midst of challenges? What strategies work for you as you seek to grow in these qualities?

PART II

BE STRONG

"Be of good comfort, Mr. Ridley, and play the man! We shall this day light such a candle, by God's grace, in England, as I trust never shall be put out."[10] Grim last words, these, grim and stirring. Nicholas Ridley and Hugh Latimer, Protestant reformers who flourished during the reign of King Edward VI, quickly fell out of favor when Edward died and his half-sister Mary, a convinced Catholic, came to the throne. Ridley had served as bishop of London and Latimer as bishop of Worcester and later chaplain to King Edward. It was an intolerant era: Protestants burned Catholics, and Catholics burned Protestants.[11] After Mary's accession, Ridley and Latimer were tried, convicted, and sentenced to death—unless they recanted. They refused, and on October 16, 1555, they were chained to the stake and burned. A Victorian-era monument in Oxford marks the spot. A later edition of John Foxe's *Book of Martyrs* records Latimer's words to Ridley as the flames rose. "Play the man!" In the face of unimaginable suffering—one report says that Ridley died very slowly and in excruciating pain—Latimer urges Ridley: Be strong.

As we saw in the previous section, Paul begins his final letter to Timothy with a backward glance. Remember your roots, Paul tells him. Remember your forebears. Remember the apostolic commission that dramatically altered the direction of your life. But quickly, Paul turns his attention to the present. In this time of transition, with the leadership torch passing from mentor to apprentice, challenges abound, internal and external. The church, then as always, struggles with conflict. The church, then as always, struggles with a hostile environment. While the details of the struggle vary from generation to generation, the principle remains the same. Leading the Christian community is hard and often dangerous work. We may not be burned at the stake, but at times our hearts burn with fear and grief. Paul writes, "I am under daily pressure because of my anxiety for all the churches" (2 Corinthians 11:28). He never downplays the difficulties nor explains them away, and in this section of 2 Timothy, he confronts the struggle head on: Be strong, Timothy. It's not going to be easy.

Nor does Jesus himself minimize the cost of following him. "If any want to become my followers, let them deny themselves and take up their cross and follow me. For those who want to save their life will lose it, and those who lose their life for my sake, and for the sake of the gospel, will save it" (Mark 8:34-35). To emphasize the cost of discipleship, Luke's Gospel offers two powerful images—a tower under construction and a king and his army facing overwhelming opponents (Luke 14:25-33). Jesus' closing words at the Last Supper include a warning: "In the world you will face persecution" (John 16:33). Nowhere does the New Testament imply that following Jesus will ever be easy. On the contrary, a decision to walk with Jesus is a decision to put ourselves in danger.

For some, the danger is literal. "When Christ calls a man, he bids him come and die," the twentieth-century martyr Dietrich Bonhoeffer wrote.[12] For others, the dangers come in subtler shapes and forms. Timothy's apostolic call will plunge him more deeply into the maelstrom of warring Christians and an increasingly antagonistic social and political environment. And so his mentor spends time early in the letter bucking up his young apprentice. Paul does not, even for a moment, encourage Timothy to make light of the hardships he will endure. But in the face of those hardships, he urges Timothy: "Be strong in the grace that is in Christ Jesus" (2 Timothy 2:1). We will do well to pay attention ourselves.

CHAPTER THREE

Truth in Advertising

Do not be ashamed, then, of the testimony about our Lord or of me his prisoner, but join with me in suffering for the gospel, relying on the power of God...You are aware that all who are in Asia have turned away from me, including Phygelus and Hermogenes. May the Lord grant mercy to the household of Onesiphorus, because he often refreshed me and was not ashamed of my chain; when he arrived in Rome, he eagerly searched for me and found me—may the Lord grant that he will find mercy from the Lord on that day! And you know very well how much service he rendered in Ephesus.

—2 Timothy 1:8, 15-18

"You never really know what curves life will throw at you, what is lurking around the corner, what is hovering above, what is swimming beneath the surface."[13] So begins a volume called *The Worst-Case Scenario Survival Handbook.* If something can go wrong, the *Handbook* tells us, it probably will. What do you do, for example, if you jump out of an airplane, pull the parachute's ripcord, and nothing happens? How do you escape from a bear, fend off a shark, wrestle yourself free from an alligator, or find shelter from a swarm of killer bees? Disasters, large and small, are everywhere, ready to strike: earthquakes, hurricanes, shipwrecks, tornadoes, avalanches. The *Handbook* does not make for peaceful bedtime reading!

Nor does Paul's second letter to Timothy. "Join with me in suffering for the gospel," writes Paul. A lay leader named Jack taught me that following Jesus will often bring us face-to-face with our own worst-case scenarios. For Jack, that scenario involved his fear of the homeless mentally ill. His church was located in the downtown section of his city, and an unusually large population of homeless mentally ill people roamed the streets near the church building. For some reason, the sight of them terrified Jack. Did they awaken fears that he too might someday have to struggle with mental illness? Or did he worry that these homeless people might suddenly accost him and make demands? Jack couldn't articulate his fear, but it almost paralyzed him. When he drove to church, he told me, he would stare straight ahead, doing his best to avoid looking at the people on the sidewalks. That was no easy task, given his church's location and the large numbers of homeless people who seemed drawn to the church almost by gravitational pull.

One day, Jack's priest called with a proposal. "Jack," Mother Pam said, "we had a vestry meeting last night and found ourselves talking about all of the homeless mentally ill people around the church. We all agreed that we need to do something for them. I mean, it seems as though Jesus has put them there just for us. So one vestry member suggested that we start a feeding program, perhaps providing one or two hot lunches per week as a start. Everyone thought that this was a great idea. And then we began asking ourselves who ought to head up a program like this. Our answer was unanimous. You!" Jack told me that he wanted to scream, "No! Anything but that! Send me as a missionary to the farthest corner of the earth. Make me stand on a street corner with a floppy black Bible and preach. Something, anything. But not that!" But instead, Jack told Mother Pam that he would pray about it. And as he prayed, Jack told me, to his utter horror, he sensed Jesus telling him to say yes to his deepest fear. He could now understand Job's agonized words: "Truly the thing that I fear comes upon me, and what I dread befalls me" (Job 3:25).

Sometimes Christians are tempted to oversell the benefits of following Jesus. That can certainly happen in the heat of evangelistic zeal. *Come to Jesus, and your relationship problems will be healed. Come to Jesus, and your financial worries are over. Come to Jesus, and your physical ailments will evaporate. Come to Jesus, and your teenagers (or your toddlers) will become compliant.* Perpetually smiling televangelists radiate good health, prosperity, and happy families: qualities that all of us desire but many do not experience. Indeed, the Bible is filled with example after example of faithful people experiencing immense hardship, broken relationships, and spiritual desolation as a result of that very faithfulness. The prophet Jeremiah, who preaches in the late seventh and early sixth centuries BCE, exemplifies this terrible reality. He faithfully proclaims God's message to the religious and political authorities of his day, and his message is met with mockery, beatings, and arrests. "O LORD, you have enticed me, and I was enticed," Jeremiah complains; "you have overpowered me, and you have prevailed. I have become a laughingstock all day long; everyone mocks me" (Jeremiah 20:7).

Paul lays out for Timothy the dangers he will face when he inherits the leadership of the young Christian church. His role as mentor requires terrible honesty: "truth in advertising." Timothy needs to know what he's getting into, however frightening it might be. Paul is not entirely negative, of course. He includes a word of hope as well as a reference to the tools that will keep Timothy strong in the face of danger, as we'll see in succeeding chapters. But dangers abound, and no Christian leader—from Timothy to the present day—can ignore them. As Benedict of Nursia warns prospective monks,

"Let the novice be told all the hard and rugged ways by which the journey to God is made."[14]

Paul begins this section with a general reminder about his own condition. "Do not be ashamed, then, of the testimony about our Lord or of me his prisoner, but join with me in suffering for the gospel, relying on the power of God" (1:8). Paul is a prisoner. We will learn later that he is in chains, a painful shackling that attaches a prisoner to the wall and leaves him perpetually stretched. Paul's situation has deteriorated significantly from the one we find at the end of the Book of Acts. As Acts comes to a close, Paul is under house arrest in Rome, free to entertain guests and share the gospel with them. "When we came into Rome, Paul was allowed to live by himself, with the soldier who was guarding him…He lived there two whole years at his own expense and welcomed all who came to him" (Acts 28:16, 30). While we don't know the details, it is clear in 2 Timothy that Paul's legal status has devolved from house arrest to a more severe form of incarceration. He is locked up, chained up, and awaiting death.

From the world's perspective, Paul is a loser. His life, like his Lord's, is coming to an ignominious end. Paul wants Timothy to see that reality plainly. But despite the chains and the disrepute that accompany them, he tells him, "Do not be ashamed." Timothy, you are to bear witness to Jesus and to me: to the suffering Lord and to his suffering apostle. The word translated "testimony" is *marturion*, the root of "martyr." Originally a *marturion* was one who gave testimony in court, reporting accurately under oath on what one knows to be true by personal observation. The New Testament appropriates the word to refer to Christian testimony. "You will receive power when the Holy Spirit has come upon you," the Risen Christ tells his disciples immediately before his ascension; "and you will be my witnesses [*martys*] in Jerusalem, in all Judea and Samaria, and to the ends of the earth" (Acts 1:8). And so Paul reminds Timothy that his testimony will point to the crucified Lord and to the imprisoned apostle, to the King and to the King's servant.

And more: "Join with me in suffering for the gospel." When Timothy takes on the burden of Christian leadership, he is to do more than bear witness to the cross. He must embrace it as well. The particular example Paul gives is personal. "You are aware that all who are in Asia have turned away from me, including Phygelus and Hermogenes." We don't have any details—and probably don't need them. The mentor is simply reminding his protégé that colleagues—not all but certainly some—will reject his leadership, as surely as many rejected Paul's. Later, as we will see, Paul mentions other disappointing characters: Hymenaeus and Philetus: Demas, Crescens, and Titus[15]; and Alexander the coppersmith, who, he claims, did him great harm (4:14). The greatest heartache for Christian leaders, in the New Testament era and in the present day, is the Body of Christ itself, with all of its interpersonal dysfunction. A glance at 1 Corinthians provides sufficient evidence that from the very beginning, Christians have devoured one another and, in particular, devoured their leaders.

That brings me to a personal theory. I call it the Law of Universal Church Types, and it goes like this. In every Christian community, small or large, whatever the denomination or theological persuasion, we will meet the same people: not literally but archetypically. These Universal Church Types appear whenever Christians gather. That can be a positive phenomenon as well as a negative one. Every community seems to include devout prayer warriors, serious students of the Bible and Christian tradition, selfless leaders, dedicated worker bees who staff the kitchen, the food pantry, the Sunday school—as well as chronic complainers, stingy donors, and unpredictable church hoppers. (By "church hopper," I mean people who never stay anywhere very long but who quickly find something they don't like and move on to a new parish.) You can't get away from these Universal Types, no matter how far you run. For example, I served one parish whose vestry included Ben, the archetypal grumpy middle-aged guy who, on general principles, voted no on every issue. He was unhappy about church finances, he complained about the music we sang on Sunday morning, and he perpetually wondered aloud about how hard the rector actually worked. When, after many years, I accepted a call to another parish, I was sad to say goodbye to a community that otherwise had been overwhelmingly loving and positive. Still, I was delighted, to be honest, to leave Ben behind. When I arrived at my new parish, however, Ben was there to meet me at the door. His name was now Harry. He was a bit younger, but everything else was the same—the same unhappiness, the same complaints, the same suspicious questions. And Paul is warning Timothy that he, too, will encounter Universal Church Types. They may not be the same people who criticized Paul, but never mind. Wherever you go, Timothy, they will be there to meet you at the door.

Paul's truth-in-advertising message sounds like sheer bad news. Why would anyone want to take on a burden so oppressive? As he continues to read Paul's final letter, Timothy will discover even more disincentives to embracing the cross of Christian leadership. But in the midst of the bad news, Paul also has some profoundly good news for Timothy.

First, Paul returns—almost, it seems, as an afterthought—to the theme of power. The last phrase of verse 8 is easily missed since Paul will quickly turn his attention in verses 9-14 to some of the central elements of faith that Timothy must strive to preserve. But the phrase captures something essential about all Christian ministry: "relying on the power of God." We have already encountered this word (*dunamis*) in the preceding verse, in Paul's spiritual triad "of power and of love and of self-discipline." Now he brings the point home.

Timothy, Paul says to his apprentice, you can't do this job on your own. You will face opposition, rejection, and the heartache that comes when the people you trust the most abandon you. You may well, in God's good time, share my fate. (Christian tradition says that Timothy dies a martyr in Ephesus in 97 CE, about thirty years after his mentor's death in Rome.) And so, Paul tells Timothy, you must rely on the power of God. Paul, reminding Timothy that he is radically dependent on God, echoes Jesus himself: "Apart from me you can do nothing" (John 15:5). Throughout his letters, Paul acknowledges the source of his power. "For the weapons of our warfare," he tells his friends in Corinth, "are not merely human, but they have divine power to destroy strongholds" (2 Corinthians 10:4). "I can do all things," Paul says, adding an important proviso, "through him who strengthens me" (Philippians 4:13). The power that Paul commends to Timothy is the power that Paul has experienced from the moment of his conversion on the road to Damascus. That power, Paul says, is yours as well.

Second, Paul encourages Timothy to remember the people who will enrich his life, as they have enriched Paul's. After the painful reference to Phygelus and Hermogenes, Paul turns his attention to the more positive example of Onesiphorus. As is so often the case when we read Paul's letters, we have to use our imagination to fill in the details. Timothy knows the specifics of the aid that Onesiphorus gave to Paul; we don't. Was his assistance financial? Did he provide what today we would call emotional support? Did he hire a lawyer for Paul in the face of the apostle's precarious legal status? Did he bring food to Paul in prison? We will never know. What is clear, however, is that Onesiphorus had reached out to Paul both in Ephesus and in Rome; that Onesiphorus, in fact, traveled to Rome to be of service to the apostle. In an era when long-distance travel was both time-consuming and dangerous, this was no small matter. As we will see later on, Paul mentions other friends who, like Onesiphorus, have also stood by him during hard times (4:11, 19-

21). In other words, Paul experiences the blessing of Christian care and support as well as the devastation of betrayal and rejection. He is never alone, never utterly abandoned.

A general principle undergirds Paul's reminder. Yes, following Jesus is hard. Truth in advertising is no mere fine print disclaimer, nor is Jesus' invitation to carry the cross simply a metaphor. But in the face of the hardships built into Christian discipleship, Jesus gives us companions. We are not meant to follow Jesus apart from the company of brothers and sisters who encourage, challenge, and sometimes correct us.

My friend and colleague David Hyndman, former rector of St. Augustine's Church in Gary, Indiana, preached a sermon a few years ago to a group of ordination candidates, focusing on the theme of "sidekickery." What, in heaven's name, is that? Hyndman begins by confessing his childhood admiration for Hopalong Cassidy, played by William Boyd in a series of movies. Hoppy cleaned up the west, tracked down bad guys, and brought them to justice. "Hopalong, of course, did not have all of his adventures alone; he shared them with sidekicks, the kind of sidekicks who would get hit by swinging saloon doors, get their feet caught in spittoons, fall in the horse trough, or get captured by nasty villains." Sidekicks, however, are not ends in themselves. They "served as a contrast to the real hero, Hopalong, but more importantly, they were fiercely loyal. In all their imperfections and peccadilloes, they stood to serve, letting Hoppy be Hoppy." This points us, David Hyndman said, to our own calling. "Ministry, at least in part, includes the art of being a sidekick…The sidekick knows that ministry must first be authenticated by others, and that call is not a reward for our own wisdom and righteousness. It rather wakes us out of sleep and sets our mature lives in motion in a direction not necessarily of our own choosing but in response to the voice of God."

In many ways, Timothy served as Paul's sidekick. In his youth and frailty, he may well have demonstrated some of the comic ineptness that Hopalong Cassidy met in his companions. But Paul reminds Timothy that being a sidekick is an ongoing process, a gift that mutates and reappears through a wondrous variety of people. And so Onesiphorus and the others named later in the letter step into that role. Even in the darkest of times, Paul tells Timothy, God sends people into our lives to share the journey with us, to help us in our weakness, and to fill in the gaps when our own strength fails. "Here, then, are some of the imperatives of sidekickery," David Hyndman concludes in his sermon: "Listen, be yourself, praise, know that you are loved, know that you are gifted, know that you are not alone, and know how you are called to action. Sidekicks comprise a revered and important calling; they are flawed, of course, and at times inept because they are recruited from the likes of us."[16]

The subtext of these verses is grim. Ministry is hard, and whenever we follow Jesus, we will meet opposition, betrayal, or worst-case scenarios: truth in advertising. But Paul sets these painful realities in the context of an infrastructure of grace. My friend Jack discovered that grace when he finally, reluctantly, said yes to God's call and agreed to lead a ministry to the homeless mentally ill. It was hard, he told me. He had to lean on God and lean on other people, and even so, he often doubted his ability to carry on. As homeless people filed into the parish hall for the first time, Jack said, his stomach twisted. "So what did you learn?" I asked him. His answer came surprisingly quickly. "I learned two things," he said. "I learned that I have nothing to fear. Even when one of these people acted out or started yelling or crying or accosting others, it was okay. We got through. And I learned something else even more important. I see Jesus in them." As he faced his own worst-case scenario, Jack discovered the power of Jesus' words. "Truly I tell you, just as you did it to one of the least of these who are members of my family, you did it to me" (Matthew 25:40).

God gives us, Paul tells Timothy, power and people, supernatural strength and surprising companions. We are never, in any ultimate sense, alone.

QUESTIONS FOR REFLECTION

1. Benedict's "hard and rugged ways" are built into the life of the Christian leader, Paul tells Timothy. What are your hard and rugged ways?

2. How is Jesus challenging you to be a witness for him? What are the difficulties associated with your particular call? What are your strategies for living faithfully in the midst of those difficulties?

3. In the Gospel of John, we hear, "Apart from me you can do nothing" (15:5). How have you experienced Jesus' power as you exercise your ministry?

4. Who are your sidekicks, the people in your life who encourage and strengthen you in your ministry? How do they do so? How have you, on your part, served as a sidekick to encourage and strengthen others?

Chapter Four

Guard the Good Treasure

[God] who saved us and called us with a holy calling, not according to our works but according to his own purpose and grace. This grace was given to us in Christ Jesus before the ages began, but it has now been revealed through the appearing of our Savior Christ Jesus, who abolished death and brought life and immortality to light through the gospel. For this gospel I was appointed a herald and an apostle and a teacher, and for this reason I suffer as I do. But I am not ashamed, for I know the one in whom I have put my trust, and I am sure that he is able to guard until that day what I have entrusted to him. Hold to the standard of sound teaching that you have heard from me, in the faith and love that are in Christ Jesus. Guard the good treasure entrusted to you, with the help of the Holy Spirit living in us.
—2 Timothy 1:9-14

"I have no idea what to do," Janice said. She had come to me for advice about her ministry. Over the years, her commitment to Jesus had deepened, her prayer life had blossomed, and she read the Bible regularly and with growing understanding. She spent her days teaching a class for severely developmentally disabled children and her late afternoons and evenings with her husband, her own children, and their unceasing round of soccer, homework, and family time. "I want to do more for Jesus," she told me, "but I'm stumped. I don't have any training, I've never been to seminary, I'm terrified of public speaking, and in any case, I don't have *time*. My days are too full." "So tell me what your days at work are like," I said. "Well, they're pretty routine," Janice replied. "The children arrive, the aides and I try to find activities that that work for them…but sometimes I sit there for hours, it seems, with a child on my lap." "And what do you do?" "Nothing, really," Janice said. "These children are nonverbal. I just sit and pray silently for them. I can't pray aloud—it's against the law, and in any case, the children wouldn't understand. Silent prayer, hour after hour, that's how I spend my days." "And that," I told Janice, "is your ministry. That's what Jesus wants you to do."

"Lay ministry" is a broad and often misunderstood term. It refers not simply to church-oriented tasks (ushering, counting money, preparing Sunday School lessons) nor even primarily to Christian outreach (from staffing a soup kitchen to participating in a short-term mission trip). *The Book of Common Prayer* has a rather "high" doctrine of the ministry of all the baptized: "The ministry of lay persons is to represent Christ and his Church; to bear witness to him wherever they may be; and, according to the gifts given them, to carry on Christ's work of reconciliation in the world; and to take their place in the life, worship, and governance of the Church."[17]

The church-oriented part of lay ministry is relegated to the end! Most lay ministry, in fact, takes place where people work, go to school, and raise their families. It is there—in our workplaces, neighborhoods, and homes—that our commitment is put to the test. It is there that we must apply our faith and make it real. And it is there that we need practical help. How do I share Jesus Christ in a secular setting? How do I impart faith to my children? How am I supposed to make my voice heard in, for example, the political arena? And how can I be sure that whatever I do or say reflects the gospel? In many ways, these questions are more challenging than any I've faced in decades of ordained ministry. But the questions point to the same quandary that all Christians, lay or clergy, struggle with every day. What tools are available to move us from a merely theoretical appreciation of the faith? What are we actually supposed to do? How do we take hold of the practical and spiritual resources that will help us to make a difference to the people we meet every day?

Timothy may well have asked the same questions. His theological formation had been superb: He had learned the Bible as a child, studied scripture at the feet of Paul, spent hours in private conversation with him, and watched his mentor in action in the midst of horrendously difficult circumstances. But now what? How was he to go about doing the same? Throughout 2 Timothy, Paul answers those questions. Above all, Paul tells Timothy, you need to be clear about the gospel and about your call.

First, Paul says, be clear about the gospel. In many of Paul's letters, he carefully and at some length spells out the heart of the Christian message, the death and resurrection of Jesus. The pastoral letters, on the other hand, focus on practical matters and lack lengthy theological discourse. Still, even in brief, Paul ticks off the essentials of the gospel. God, he says, "saved us and called us with a holy calling, not according to our works but according to his own purpose and grace. This grace was given to us in Christ Jesus before the ages began, but it has now been revealed through the appearing of our Savior Christ Jesus, who abolished death and brought life and immortality to light through the gospel." This is a bullet-point summary intended to keep Timothy grounded in what's really important: We've been rescued from sin and death and summoned into a life of service. Why? Not because of any particular merit of ours but because we are the objects of the love of the God of the universe. Indeed, Paul is telling Timothy, from before time began—before the Big Bang, before history as we know it, before

Paul or Timothy had been born—that God has intended to lavish love upon us. And now God has done it. Jesus has come, death is abolished, and we are transformed. This, Paul says, is the heart of the gospel. While Paul does not specifically mention the cross or the empty tomb, they are implied in the result. Jesus is the savior, the rescuer. His death and resurrection have "brought life and immortality to light." In the midst of this thoroughly practical letter, mentor to apprentice, Paul urges Timothy to cling to the heart of the gospel.

We too must cling to that heart. The Christian faith, Joseph Ratzinger (Pope Benedict XVI) reminds us, includes nonnegotiable claims: about who Jesus is, about the shape of the Christian life, about our response to Jesus' gracious invitation. Like Paul before him, Pope Benedict lays out a kind of irreducible minimum:

> [E]very statement about the Faith is ordered to the four basic elements: the *Creed*, the *Our Father*, the *Decalogue*, and the *sacraments*. The whole foundation of Christian life is thereby included—the synthesis of the Church's teaching as it is based on Scripture and Tradition. Christians find here what they are to *believe* (the Symbolum or Creed), what they are to *hope* (the Our Father), what they are to *do* (the Decalogue or Ten Commandments), and the ambience in which all this is to be accomplished (the sacraments).[18]

Timothy, Paul says, you must never lose sight of the cosmos-altering events, the unchanging truths that stand at the center of our faith. They will shape your ministry, guide your teaching, and strengthen you beyond measure in moments of overwhelming darkness.

Second, Paul says, be clear about your call. He makes this point by looking at his own apostolic commission: "For this gospel I was appointed a herald and an apostle and a teacher, and for this reason I suffer as I do. But I am not ashamed, for I know the one in whom I have put my trust, and I am sure that he is able to guard until that day what I have entrusted to him." Paul lifts into the light, like facets of a diamond, three elements of his call. He is, to begin with, a herald. The Greek word, *kerux*, refers to an official who stands in a public place and reads an announcement from the governing authorities. In the same way, Paul—and Timothy after him—is to make an announcement from God, our king: Jesus Christ died for our sins, has risen from the dead, and now reigns in glory.

Paul is, as well, an apostle, *apostolos*, one who is sent. The word first referred to Jesus' inner circle of disciples, the Twelve. Over time the term has come to be used more broadly, pointing to others whose calling involved a sending. "Greet Andronicus and Junia, my relatives, who were in prison with me," he writes the Christians in Rome; "they are prominent among the apostles" (Romans 16:7). Paul regularly identifies himself as an apostle (Romans 1:1; 1 Corinthians 1:1; 2 Corinthians 1:1, 12:12; among many references), and some interpreters maintain that Paul is the true replacement for the traitor Judas. Matthias, they believe, was hastily and perhaps overeagerly appointed to fill the empty slot in the apostolic college (Acts 1:15-26), and only later was the real replacement identified. Whatever the case, Paul's ministry is apostolic par excellence. "While [the Christians in Antioch] were worshiping the Lord and fasting, the Holy Spirit said, 'Set apart for me Barnabas and Saul for the work to which I have called them.' Then, after fasting and praying they laid their hands on them and sent them off" (Acts 13:2-3). Sent he was: to Cyprus, Asia (modern day Turkey), Greece, and Rome. Soon Timothy will take up Paul's apostolic mantle. He too will be sent.

Finally, Paul identifies himself as a teacher. The underlying Greek word, *didaskalos*, points to the systematic presentation of material. A herald proclaims the message, while a teacher explains it. Here's what the message means, the teacher says, and here is how it applies to your life. In Antioch, long before he began his missionary travels, Paul and his companion Barnabas spend an entire year teaching the church (Acts 11:26). Much later, we catch a comic glimpse of Paul's teaching ministry during his third missionary journey, as he passes through Troas on the western coast of modern-day Turkey.

> When we met to break bread, Paul was holding a discussion
> with them; since he intended to leave the next day, he continued
> speaking until midnight. There were many lamps in the
> room upstairs where we were meeting. A young man named
> Eutychus, who was sitting in the window, began to sink off into
> a deep sleep while Paul talked still longer. Overcome by sleep,
> he fell to the ground three floors below and was picked up dead.
> But Paul went down, and bending over him took him in his
> arms and said, "Do not be alarmed, for his life is in him." Then
> Paul went upstairs, and after he had broken bread and eaten, he
> continued to converse with them until dawn. —Acts 20:7-11

From first to last, Paul explains the faith that he proclaims and does so, apparently, at great length. At the same time, he is absolutely clear about the breadth of his call. He knows what Jesus has asked him to do, a triad of roles that shape his ministry from the moment of his encounter with Jesus on the Damascus road until, years later in a Roman prison cell, he awaits the executioner's ax. Paul never forgets that the Lord has made him a herald, an apostle, and a teacher.

Paul's sense of call is not simply a theoretical concept. When he says "I was appointed," the phrase implies the story that undergirds his ministry: the story of his early years as a persecutor of the church, his dramatic conversion, the restoration of his eyesight when Ananias addresses him as Brother Saul, his first attempts to preach his new faith, the years of waiting, the summons to join Barnabas in Antioch, and finally the prophetic utterance that sends him careening into the Roman world. That story appears in narrative form three times in the Book of Acts (chapters 9, 22, and 26), and Paul himself regularly alludes to it (1 Corinthians 9:1; 15:8-9; Galatians 1:13-17). He is a herald, an apostle, and a teacher because Jesus intervenes in his life and saves him from himself. Although

Paul knows that his story will include martyrdom, he is equally certain of the final result. It is both personal ("I know the one in whom I have put my trust") and providential ("he is able to guard until that day what I have entrusted to him"). Jesus is in charge of the Big Story, one that will extend far beyond Paul's earthly life.

Timothy, too, has a narrative, though the details are sketchy, as we've seen: a Christian mother and grandmother; meeting Paul; and an invitation to serve Paul as traveling companion and assistant. When Paul outlines his call, one that emerges from a powerful story, he is encouraging Timothy to identify his own call and the story that makes it possible. Timothy, after all, is about to inherit not simply the mantle of leadership but also the burdens that accompany it. In the face of your new role, Paul tells Timothy, you too must be clear about what Jesus is asking you to do.

Clarity about call can be negative as well as positive. In 1997, for example, Trinity Episcopal School for Ministry in Ambridge, Pennsylvania, invited me to consider coming to the seminary to teach pastoral theology. I found the offer enormously attractive. By that time, I had been ordained twenty-six years, and the notion of mentoring future generations of leaders was profoundly intriguing. On the other hand, I was a happy parish priest with a flourishing congregation (All Saints Church in Bakersfield, California). What does Jesus want? After a good deal of internal struggle (two weeks' worth), I finally called the seminary and said yes. And so, with mixed emotions, I gathered the parish vestry and turned in my resignation. The next day, by accident of calendar, I traveled to the east coast for a meeting, and as I left the airplane and walked down the jet bridge, it felt as though I slammed against a wall. The feeling was almost physical, and I could almost hear a voice saying: "Don't You Dare." It was a moment almost as numinous and as disturbing as the encounter, a couple of decades earlier, in the field behind St. Joseph's, as related in Chapter Two. I hedge this around with the word "almost" because the experience was somewhere between audible/tactile and internal/intuitive. Whatever had happened, I knew that I wasn't meant to go to Ambridge, that God still had work for me to do in the parish, and that my ministry—in whatever form—was to be primarily pastoral. I quickly called my bishop and my senior warden (lay president of the parish) and "un-resigned." They and the vestry graciously took me back. I also had to make a painful phone call to Trinity's dean and withdraw my acceptance. It was a terrible, embarrassing, and profoundly humbling time, in which God's no undid my flawed yes. But this incident also, despite the pain, helped me to clarify my call and what it was God was asking me to do and be.[19]

Third, Paul says, be clear about the burden you've undertaken. His words at this point turn both solemn and hopeful: solemn, because Timothy is to become a steward of an infinitely precious gift; hopeful, because God is both the source and the power that will sustain him. The burden itself is twofold. To begin with, Paul tells Timothy to "hold to the standard of sound teaching." The word translated to "standard," *hypotyposis*, means something like an outline or sketch. In other words, Paul has given Timothy a solid outline of the faith. That outline is to form the basis for all of Timothy's subsequent teaching—much as, for example, the Apostles' Creed can provide a series of scripturally based bullet points for a teacher to "flesh out," filling in the details, explaining the nuances, applying doctrine to contemporary life. The starting point, however, is the standard or outline, the bedrock that must undergird all teaching.

Timothy's burden as Paul's successor includes an additional and even more serious task. He is to "guard the good treasure." The 1928 *Book of Common Prayer* includes a reminder that bishops are to "banish and drive away from the Church all erroneous and strange doctrine contrary to God's Word."[20] While the church has sometimes, and tragically, taken this charge to grim excess, it is equally disastrous to treat Christian doctrine as infinitely pliable.

Paul is asking Timothy to remember that he didn't invent the gospel; rather, he received it. And now his burden is to protect the gospel from false teaching, as he in turn passes it on to the next generation of believers.

Even in the New Testament era, Christians were tempted to add to, or subtract from, the gospel. Paul himself, for example, goes to battle with ceremonial legalists in his letter to the Galatians, with resurrection-deniers in 1 Corinthians 15, and with end-time enthusiasts in 1 and 2 Thessalonians. The three letters bearing the name of John respond to false teachers who "do not confess that Jesus Christ has come in the flesh" (2 John 7). And the Book of Revelation opens with a series of letters in which Jesus takes churches to task for both moral and theological lapses. In other words, being serious about Christian teaching and guarding it from distortion stand at the heart of apostolic ministry. A Christian leader must never present an idiosyncratic message. Yes, the message should be conveyed creatively, winsomely, and in a culturally appropriate manner but always, Paul reminds Timothy, faithfully. Christians must resist the twin dangers of reductionism (leaving out the unpleasant, uncongenial, or challenging aspects of the gospel) and expansionism (adding extraneous material which weakens or waters down the gospel's pressing message). Screwtape, C. S. Lewis' diabolical mentor, advises his apprentice demon Wormwood to employ expansionism as a way of drawing a new Christian away from God:

> The real trouble about the set your patient [the young Christian whom Wormwood is trying to tempt] is living in is that it is *merely* Christian. They all have individual interests, of course, but the bond remains mere Christianity. What we want, if men become Christians at all, is to keep them in the state of mind I call "Christianity And". You know—Christianity and the Crisis, Christianity and the New Psychology, Christianity and the New Order, Christianity and Faith Healing, Christianity and Psychical Research, Christianity and Vegetarianism,

Christianity and Spelling Reform. If they must be Christians let them at least be Christians with a difference. Substitute for the faith some Fashion with a Christian coloring. Work on their horror of the Same Old Thing. The horror of the Same Old Thing is one of the most valuable passions we have produced in the human heart—an endless source of heresies in religion, folly in counsel, infidelity in marriage, and inconstancy in friendship.[21]

Happily, Paul's twofold charge to "hold to the standard" and "guard the good treasure" includes the gift without which all Christian ministry will fail: "with the help of the Holy Spirit living in us" (verse 14). Jesus never sends us out unaided. As Timothy embraces the burden of his apostolic call, Jesus' promise before his ascension will sustain him: "You will receive power when the Holy Spirit has come upon you; and you will be my witnesses" (Acts 1:8). That same promise sustains us.

QUESTIONS FOR REFLECTION

1. If you were asked to summarize the heart of the gospel, how would you do it? What is essential? What is peripheral? How do you distinguish the one from the other?

2. Paul was clear about his call as herald, apostle, and teacher. What images or roles can you use to describe your own call?

3. Paul's sense of call comes through the story of his conversion and his missionary journeys. How has your story helped you to understand God's call?

4. When have you misheard God's call? How did you discover your mistake, and what helped you to make a mid-course correction?

CHAPTER FIVE

Unchained

You then, my child, be strong in the grace that is in Christ Jesus; and what you have heard from me through many witnesses entrust to faithful people who will be able to teach others as well. Share in suffering like a good soldier of Christ Jesus. No one serving in the army gets entangled in everyday affairs; the soldier's aim is to please the enlisting officer. And in the case of an athlete, no one is crowned without competing according to the rules. It is the farmer who does the work who ought to have the first share of the crops. Think over what I say, for the Lord will give you understanding in all things.

Remember Jesus Christ, raised from the dead, a descendant of David—that is my gospel, for which I suffer hardship, even to the point of being chained like a criminal. But the word of God is not chained. Therefore I endure everything for the sake of the elect, so that they may also obtain the salvation that is in Christ Jesus, with eternal glory. The saying is sure: If we have died with him, we will also live with him; if we endure, we will also reign with him; if we deny him, he will also deny us; if we are faithless, he remains faithful— for he cannot deny himself.

—2 Timothy 2:1-13

Chuck. More than sixty years after he passed out of my life, his name still frightens me. He was the quintessential playground bully: unnaturally large, with enormous, muscled arms and hands so huge that one could mistake them for baseball mitts. He had an instinct for identifying the most vulnerable kid on the playground and making that kid's life miserable. More often than not, I was that kid. I recently found a stash of old eight-millimeter films, taken during my elementary school years, and had them turned into a DVD, and there, at a fifth-grade, end-of-school-year party, was Chuck—as terrifying now on my computer screen as he was when I did everything in my power to avoid him on the playground. One day, for example, I pleaded with the teacher to let me stay inside and clean the erasers instead of joining my classmates outside. "But why?" she asked. "It's a beautiful day out there!" In that vulnerable moment, I confessed that Chuck terrified me. My teacher seemed flummoxed. This was 1957, after all, decades away from our culture's current awareness of bullies. "Oh," she said, "just go out there and…and be strong. Be strong." Unhelpful words, these.

Does Timothy find the words of his mentor equally unhelpful? "You then, my child, be strong in the grace that is in Christ Jesus." It's true that Paul tempers his command with two important modifiers. Timothy's strength is to be in grace (that is, in God's unconditional favor toward us) and in Jesus. But as he prepares for the enormous task he's about to undertake—leading the church in its post-Pauline phase and in the chaos of internal conflict and external opposition—precisely how is he to be strong? What can he expect God to provide him? The phrase translated "be strong" is derived from *dunamis* (which we encountered earlier), the root of our word "dynamite," and the concept of God's empowering grace is scattered throughout the New Testament, from Jesus' promise in Acts 1:8 to Paul's audacious claim in Philippians 4:13. But what does supernatural strength actually look like? Is it physical, a kind of Spirit-empowered brute force? Or is it emotional, the ability to stand unwavering in the face of relentless opposition? These questions are as pertinent to us as they were to Timothy. Whatever task we undertake, as Christian parents or Christian teachers or Christian leaders or Christian caregivers or Christian citizens, how can we expect the Lord to strengthen us?

Paul offers Timothy four elements of supernatural strength. None of them is easy. All involve, in larger or smaller ways, embracing the cross (see Luke 9:23 and its parallels). And in all of them, Timothy will be empowered to follow Jesus.

First, Timothy will have strength to let go. "What you have heard from me through many witnesses entrust to faithful people who will be able to teach others as well." Paul reminds his apprentice that Timothy himself is a temporary fixture. Even though he has not yet taken Paul's place, Timothy should be thinking about his own successors. His job is not simply to identify people who understand the faith. No, he is to find leaders who themselves can commend the faith to the next generation after them. Timothy, after all, will someday pass from the scene. Who will take his place? The process of mentoring is always multigenerational and never-ending. Christian leadership, at its most profound, involves letting go of leadership, making provision for the future, and ensuring that the gospel will continue to find strong, articulate, and winsome voices. And so Paul urges Timothy, at this early stage, to cast his eye around the church in search of apt teachers. Note that Paul doesn't narrow the task. Teachers come in many styles and shapes: those who lecture, those who like Socrates help learners to discover truth they already know, those whose lives more than their words embody the gospel. Timothy is free to gaze across the spectrum of the church and seek a wide variety of teachers to succeed him. He is not free, however, to hold on to his apostolic ministry in perpetuity. Like Paul, he must let go. Was that a painful reality for him?

I met George Arthur Buttrick in the fall of 1969; he was seventy-eight years old and a retired Presbyterian minister. A world-famous mid-twentieth century preacher, he also wrote prolifically and served as editor of *The Interpreter's Bible* and *The Interpreter's Dictionary of the Bible*. By the time I encountered him, he was teaching homiletics as a retirement assignment at Garrett Theological Seminary in Evanston, Illinois, across the street from my own school, Seabury-Western Theological Seminary. Because Seabury and Garrett had a cross-registration arrangement, I decided to enroll in Dr. Buttrick's introduction to preaching course, and my life changed forever. Even at a distance of fifty years, I can still hear his voice—a soft British accent—and see him standing in the pulpit of the Garrett chapel. Even now, so many decades later, I read his lecture notes and recognize that he still shapes my vision for preaching. I remember evenings in his home, where he entertained seminarians with his "war stories" and answered endless questions about the task of preaching. I can still hold in my hands the sermon outlines that he critiqued (sometimes quite harshly), his red-inked comments sharp and concise. In his only volume of published sermons, he summarized the preacher's work: "Preaching is never to people in general or to a crowd at large but to an individual group or church. Only the pastor, or a man with pastoral imagination, can preach."[22] George Buttrick shaped a generation of Christian leaders, and I am grateful beyond words to be numbered among them. I am, of course, no George Buttrick; his unique personality and gifts are unrepeatable. But the preaching ministry I exercise today bears the imprint of his mentoring.[23] In the last years of his ministry, Dr. Buttrick embodied 2 Timothy 2:2. He let go and empowered others.

Second, Timothy will have strength to suffer, a return to the theme of truth in advertising. Paul makes this point with three back-to-back images. A Christian leader, he says, is like a soldier, an athlete, and a farmer. Each picture points to an element, a painful element, of leadership.

Soldiers, for example, must avoid civilian entanglements and obey those placed above them in the chain of command. The New

Testament often uses a soldierly analogy to describe Christian discipleship. Jesus commends a Roman centurion (essentially a company captain) who has asked him to heal his servant. The centurion is well aware of military protocol. "Lord, I am not worthy to have you come under my roof," he told Jesus; "but only speak the word, and my servant will be healed. For I also am a man under authority, with soldiers under me; and I say to one, 'Go,' and he goes, and to another, 'Come,' and he comes, and to my slave, 'Do this,' and the slave does it." Jesus responds enthusiastically, "Truly I tell you, in no one in Israel have I found such faith" (Matthew 8:8-10). A soldier's readiness to obey, then, is a model of Christian obedience. We, like the soldier, must be predisposed to say yes— to Jesus. Elsewhere in the New Testament, a military analogy is employed to encourage faithful, fearless, and costly discipleship (1 Corinthians 9:7; 2 Corinthians 10:4; Ephesians 6:10-17). Yes, these images can be misused; Christian aggression (such as the bloody Crusades of the Middle Ages) haunts the church. But the truth behind the analogy is the soldier's single-minded focus. Timothy, Paul is saying, keep your eyes fixed on Jesus. Avoid distractions that will draw you away from your apostolic task. Listen for the voice of Jesus and, when he calls, be ready to answer. The disciple's default, like the soldier's, is obedience.

Athletes, Paul reminds Timothy, play by the rules in order to win the crown (the ancient equivalent of a gold medal; see also 1 Corinthians 9:24-27). If you're a javelin-thrower, you must release your javelin from a particular spot if your shot is to count. If you're a runner, you must begin at the starting block and end at the finish line. If you're a wrestler, you must follow the protocols of your sport if you hope to be declared the winner. In other words, athletes submit to a kind of voluntary self-limitation: you can do X but not Y or Z. Disciples, too, must voluntarily limit themselves. Jesus' painfully challenging words in the Sermon on the Mount (Matthew 5-7) are a case in point. In his first "discipleship training speech," Jesus tells his followers to avoid anger, lust, revenge, easy oath-taking, attention-grabbing piety, acquisitiveness, and crippling worry. It's easier to list these prohibited behaviors than to avoid them! The point, however, is that there is a significant parallel between the athlete's decision to play by the rules and a disciple's decision to fashion his or her life according to the New Testament's demanding standards. Of course, we regularly fail. "If we say that we have no sin, we deceive ourselves, and the truth is not in us" (1 John 1:8). But the disciple, like the athlete, never ceases to strive—always aware of our dependence upon grace.

Farmers, Paul adds, work hard. My father-in-law showed me what this means. Raised on an Iowa farm, he married a California girl during World War II and, in the 1950s, bought a plot of land in the Coachella Valley, bleak desert country running southeast from the resort of Palm Springs. While I didn't meet Bill Gardner until the mid-1960s, when his citrus ranch was already producing oranges, tangerines, tangelos, lemons, and grapefruit, I can imagine the immense task he faced: irrigating the desert, facing scorching heat in the summer and occasional hard freezes in the winter, tending and pruning trees in a hostile environment, coaxing a crop from ground where no crop should grow. He was, par excellence, "the farmer who does the work." Timothy, Paul tells his young apprentice, you too will work very, very hard: long days, relentless pressure, no time off because "the fields are ripe for harvesting" (John 4:35), a task infinitely more immense than the one facing Bill Gardner when he decided to bring life to a lifeless desert. Yes, discipleship—following the example of Jesus himself (Mark 1:35)—involves times of rest and refreshment alternating with extreme exertion, but here Paul stresses the "exertion" side of the equation. When you take on the mantle of leadership, he says to Timothy, brace yourself for hard work.

Paul piles these images one on top of the other in rapid succession to make a single point to Timothy. You will suffer. The work is hard. It will demand obedience, focus, and extraordinary effort.

Third, Timothy will have strength to endure. Not only is ministry hard but also it is a long-haul commitment, stretching over years and decades, rather than merely weeks and months. How is he to maintain the energy and the pace to survive the opposition and disappointment that will inevitably come his way? How is he to keep on keeping on? To begin with, Paul urges Timothy to remember who Jesus is—"raised from the dead, a descendant of David." Here Paul summarizes an earlier teaching concerning Jesus, "who was descended from David according to the flesh and was declared to be Son of God with power according to the spirit of holiness by resurrection from the dead" (Romans 1:3-4). When your work drags on and on, Timothy, remember that you follow a Lord who is at once fully human and fully divine. Nearly four centuries later, at the Council of Chalcedon, the church would "acknowledge one and the same Son, our Lord Jesus Christ, at once complete in Godhead and complete in manhood, truly God and truly man,"[24] but the roots of that affirmation are here, in Paul's word of encouragement to Timothy. Jesus, Paul says, shares DNA with his ancestor David, Israel's great (and flawed) king, and Jesus, Paul says, enjoys an utterly unique relationship with God the Father, to which his resurrection attests. Even at this early stage in the life of the church, Christians recognize in Jesus the one who is both our brother and our Lord. Remember Jesus Christ, Paul says.

More than that, remember what Jesus promises us. Although Paul is, quite literally in chains, "…the word of God is not chained." Paul points to a promise: When we're faithful to our call, the Lord will accomplish his purposes. This doesn't mean a trouble-free life. Far from it! But Paul experiences, over and over, how Jesus uses even his troubles as a vehicle to proclaim the gospel. The Book of Acts, for example, ends at an earlier stage of Paul's captivity in Rome, when he is under what we would call house arrest. His circumstances are not as grim as those he faces when he writes 2 Timothy, but his freedom is severely limited. Still, he "lived there [under house arrest] two whole years at his own expense and welcomed all who came to him, proclaiming the kingdom of God and teaching about the Lord Jesus Christ with all boldness and without hindrance" (Acts 28:30-31).

I have always felt a special attachment to Samuel Isaac Joseph Schereschewsky, in large part because he and I share the distinction of being two of just three Anglican bishops of Lithuanian Jewish extraction (Bishop Geralyn Wolf, formerly bishop of Rhode Island, is the third). Converted to Christianity in 1855, he was ordained four years later and served as a missionary in China, eventually becoming bishop of Shanghai in 1877. In declining health, he resigned his episcopal ministry in 1883 and devoted the rest of his life to translating the Bible. Although "paralyzed in every limb, and with his powers of speech partly gone, [he sat] for nearly twenty-five years in the same chair, slowly and painfully typing out with two fingers his Mandarin translation of the Old Testament and Easy Wen-li translation of the whole Bible."[25] During my years in seminary, my assigned seat in choir faced a stained-glass window of this courageous and faithful disciple whose life, even in weakness, embodied the power of the gospel. Unchained indeed.

Nor should Timothy forget why we do what we do. "I endure everything," Paul reminds Timothy, "for the sake of the elect, so that they may also obtain the salvation that is in Christ Jesus, with eternal glory." For centuries, Christians have argued over the word "elect." Does it refer to predestination, an inevitability that removes free will in favor of God's sovereign action, drawing us to himself (or even more grimly, consigning some in advance to eternal damnation)? Or is it instead simply the recognition that God knows beforehand who will say yes and who will say no? Whatever it means to be chosen, Paul's point is clear. Timothy must never forget that his apostolic ministry is not for his own sake. It is for the sake of those who have not yet responded to the gospel. "The church is the only institution that exists primarily for the benefit of those who are not its members," says a quote often ascribed to Archbishop of Canterbury William Temple.[26] Why should Paul and Timothy endure? Not to prove their own persistence, nor to demonstrate their holiness. Not to carry out some sort of ecclesiastical game plan, nor to build up the institutional structures of the church. Rather, Paul tells his apprentice, Timothy is to bend heart and mind, soul and spirit, to one end: that others may come to know, love, and follow Jesus Christ.

Fourth, Timothy will have strength to believe in the face of hardship. Many commentators suggest that Paul is citing a few lines from an early Christian hymn. The text has a kind of rhythmic quality, and one can imagine singing these words. Whatever the case, Paul is proclaiming Jesus' faithfulness. "If we have died with him," Paul says, "we will also live with him," a phrase which echoes his earlier teaching on baptism in Romans (6:3-5). As we have been plunged into the tomb-like waters of baptism, so we—like Jesus—will burst from the tomb, walking "in newness of life," some day to be "united with him in a resurrection like his." However grim the challenges we face, Jesus will be absolutely faithful to his promise. "If we endure, we will also reign with him." Paul's words (or the song?) anticipate the final victory at the end of time, when "the kingdom of the world has become the kingdom of our Lord and of his Messiah, and he will reign forever and ever" (Revelation 11:15), and we ourselves are transformed into "a kingdom and priests serving our God, and they will reign on earth" (Revelation 5:10). Paul encourages Timothy, as he prepares to assume apostolic leadership, to remember the big picture, the divine plan that extends through time and beyond.

The final lines of this hymn appear, at first glance, to contradict themselves. Initially, Paul seems to stress the negative result of saying no to Jesus: "If we deny him, he will also deny us." Jesus himself had made the same point. "Whoever denies me before others will be denied before the angels of God" (Luke 12:9). But "if we are faithless," Paul adds, "he remains faithful—for he cannot deny himself." Our no is not, after all, the last word. Paul's own conversion stands forever as testimony to this reality! The Pharisee Saul says no and no and no and no, and on the Damascus road, Jesus transforms him forever. Paul's no becomes yes.

As an unchurched ninth-grader, socially awkward and seeking some sort of purpose for my life, I listened to Billy Graham in secret. Every Sunday evening, a local radio station aired Billy's Hour of Decision program with its unvarying format: a couple of gospel hymns sung by George Beverly Shea and a short sermon from the great evangelist. Week after week, I'd sneak up into my bedroom, close the door, turn off the lights, lie in bed, turn on the radio, and listen, the sound so low that it was only barely audible. I didn't want anyone, particularly my family, to know that I might be interested in…well, God. One night, toward the end of his sermon, Billy Graham said something like this: "If you're lying in your bed in the dark listening to me, I'm speaking to you." He certainly had my attention! "I want you to do something," Billy Graham went on. I waited with pounding heart, wondering what Billy would ask me to do. "I want you to get out of bed," Billy Graham said, "and kneel down on the floor and say a prayer with me, asking Jesus into your life." I thought for a moment, sat up in bed, switched off the radio, and said (in effect), "No." Billy Graham—and Jesus—were asking too much. A vague and comforting God was fine. But if I gave myself to Jesus, who knew what might happen? My no was as definite, and as final, as I could utter. That, I thought, was that.

"If we are faithless, he remains faithful." But my no, it turns out, was not as final as I imagined. Five years later, in the spring semester of my sophomore year in college, my no became a yes.[27] Jesus, it turned out, had the final word. And so Paul is not contradicting himself in these two verses. Rather, he's lifting up two sides of a theological coin. If we utterly, absolutely insist that we will have nothing to do with Jesus, Jesus will honor that choice. On the other hand, even when we refuse him most vigorously, he stretches out his hand to us, drawing us (if we give him an opening) into his heart. He is infinitely capable of transforming our temporal no into an eternal yes. Keep that in mind, Paul reminds Timothy, in the midst of your struggles. Sing of God's faithfulness, and find your strength in him.

QUESTIONS FOR REFLECTION

1. How have you let go of a ministry and helped another Christian to assume leadership? How did it feel to relinquish that ministry?

2. Paul tells Timothy that obedience, discipline, and hard work are essential components of ministry. How have you responded to the overwhelming demands of ministry? What happens when those demands seem to exceed your abilities or strength?

3. Paul endures "for the sake of the elect." What motivates you to serve? What inspires you to endure in the face of hardships?

4. Can you think of a time when you said no to Jesus? What was the result? Did a time come when your no was transformed to yes? How did that happen?

PART III

GUIDE THE FLOCK

Only once in my sixteen years as a diocesan bishop did I ordain a priest using the ordination rite found in the 1928 *Book of Common Prayer*. The ordinand, though from my diocese, served a parish in another diocese—a parish that, with its bishop's permission, worshiped exclusively with the earlier prayer book. And so I agreed to follow the parish custom and use the 1928 rite for the ordination liturgy. It was a doubly terrifying experience. The first terror was simply linguistic. Although I love traditional English with its elegant cadences, its sonorous phrases, and its long and leisurely sentences, it was another matter entirely to wrap my tongue around those words. I practiced the liturgy out loud, over and over, praying that when I presided, the words would flow effortlessly. Happily, the prayer was amply and graciously answered.

The second terror was not so easily overcome. I struggled with a spiritual terror. The 1928 ordination rite articulates a frighteningly robust understanding of the burden of priestly ministry. The ordination rites in the current *Book of Common Prayer* are clear, concise, and powerful in their simplicity. Its 1928 forebear, on the other hand, is somewhat fuller in presenting ordained ministry as a call to be answered in fear and trembling. In the 1928 version, just before hands are laid on the new priests, the bishop addresses the ordination candidates in a multi-page exhortation. The bishop reminds them of the high responsibility of their office and sternly warns them to think twice about what they are undertaking. It almost seems as though the bishop is trying to convince the ordinands to cancel the whole thing! The bishop says:

> And now again we exhort you, in the Name of our Lord Jesus Christ, that ye have in remembrance, into how high a Dignity, and to how weighty an Office and Charge ye are called: that is to say, to be Messengers, Watchmen, and Stewards of the Lord; to teach and to premonish, to feed and provide for the Lord's family; to seek for Christ's sheep that are dispersed abroad, and for his children who are in the midst of this naughty world, that they may be saved through Christ for ever. Have always therefore imprinted in your remembrance, how great a treasure is committed to your charge. For they are the sheep of Christ, which he bought with his death, and for whom he shed his blood. The Church and Congregation whom you must serve, is his Spouse, and his Body. *And if it shall happen that the same Church, or any Member thereof, do take any hurt or hindrance by reason of your negligence, ye know the greatness of the fault, and also the horrible punishment that will ensue.*[28]

Frightening words, these. How could I, or anyone, live up to that difficult challenge? As I prepared to say those words aloud, I found myself thinking back through my life as a parish priest and diocesan bishop. I remembered pastoral failures as well as pastoral victories, recalling people whom I had let down and parishes I had disappointed. The bishop's grim words do not apply solely to those called to priestly ministry, of course. Everyone in Christian leadership, lay and ordained, must take them to heart. We are all accountable. The Baptismal Covenant—reaffirmed every time a baptism is celebrated—is as challenging as the bishop's exhortation. "Will you continue in the apostles' teaching and fellowship… persevere in resisting evil… proclaim by word and example the Good News…seek and serve Christ in all persons …strive for justice and peace?"[29] Saying yes to Jesus, whatever the ministry, is a fearsome thing: When we answer Jesus' call, a burden is laid on our shoulders. "From everyone to whom much has been given," he told his disciples, "much will be required; and from the one to whom much has been entrusted, even more will be demanded" (Luke 12:48).

The bishop's exhortation and the Baptismal Covenant could easily have flowed from the pen of the apostle Paul. As he continues his own apostolic exhortation to his successor, Paul directs Timothy's attention to the burden that he is about to undertake. In his new role as a leader, Timothy will be a shepherd, a pastor, and a guide, with responsibility for "Christ's sheep that are dispersed abroad." How is Timothy to prepare himself for this task? What skills should he seek to acquire? What cast of heart and mind should he cultivate? How should he prepare his soul and spirit to care for God's people, to nourish them, and to protect them from danger?

CHAPTER SIX

The Leader's Words

Remind them of this, and warn them before God that they are to avoid wrangling over words, which does no good but only ruins those who are listening. Do your best to present yourself to God as one approved by him, a worker who has no need to be ashamed, rightly explaining the word of truth. Avoid profane chatter, for it will lead people into more and more impiety, and their talk will spread like gangrene. Among them are Hymenaeus and Philetus, who have swerved from the truth by claiming that the resurrection has already taken place. They are upsetting the faith of some. But God's firm foundation stands, bearing this inscription: "The Lord knows those who are his," and, "Let everyone who calls on the name of the Lord turn away from wickedness."

—2 Timothy 2:14-19

"Words, words, words, I'm so sick of words," Eliza Doolittle sings in *My Fair Lady*. The complaint is fair enough. We are all drowning in a sea of words. If you're like me, words engulf you from the moment you awake. In my case, a TV news channel babbles while my coffee brews. Words flow into my inbox, fill my Facebook feed with drivel, and accompany me throughout the day. Telemarketers hound me from morning to night, insistent words demanding my attention and my money. Yes, words can minister grace. "A word fitly spoken is like apples of gold in a setting of silver" (Proverbs 25:11). But they can also wither, confuse, and destroy. "No one can tame the tongue," James warns. It is "a restless evil, full of deadly poison. With it we bless the Lord and Father, and with it we curse those who are made in the likeness of God. From the same mouth come blessing and cursing" (James 3:8-10). The ability to speak, to put thoughts into words, is a uniquely human gift—one that comes with a warning. It can be dreadfully misused. James tells us to be "quick to listen, slow to speak," (James 1:19). The warning is particularly apt for those called to Christian leadership. What we say and how we say it can touch people's lives forever. Our words have the power to heal, to encourage, to empower—and to destroy.

Timothy will soon take on the burden of apostolic leadership. He will shepherd the young church through the next decades of its development and face a dizzying variety of responses to the gospel message, from bland disinterest to grim hostility. How can he find words that are at once apt and life-giving—and that honor Christ? And how can he avoid the shoals of misspoken, negative, or destructive words? Paul turns his attention, and Timothy's, to the danger of words, and to the potential of words to build up the kingdom of God.

First, Paul says, be cautious about words. "Warn [your fellow Christians] before God that they are to avoid wrangling over words, which does no good but only ruins those who are listening." "Wrangling over words" translates from the Greek *logomacheo*, which has to do with warfare: going to battle, even when the stakes aren't high, simply for the satisfaction of being right and defeating an opponent. Sadly, Christians often love to fight. We turn back to C.S. Lewis's Screwtape, who counsels Wormwood to direct his "patient's" attention to unimportant questions: "The real fun is working up hatred between those who *say* 'mass' and those who *say* 'holy communion' when neither party could possibly state the difference between, say, Hooker's doctrine and Thomas Aquinas's, in any form that would hold water for five minutes."[30]

Whether the issues are great or small, the history of the church is littered with conflict over words. At this point in 2 Timothy, Paul is pointing to the danger of minor disputes that can spiral out of control. It is easier to fight over inconsequential issues than to focus on what's truly essential. "For the kingdom of God," Paul told the Christians in Rome, "is not food and drink but righteousness and peace and joy in the Holy Spirit" (Romans 14:17). Tragically, Christians have often acted as though "food and drink" issues merited pitched battles and the spiritual casualties.

Wrangling over words has, if anything, intensified in our era. Email and the various iterations of social media make it increasingly difficult to engage in measured conversation. Words on a computer screen seem somehow harsher than those spoken face to face. When you key your anger into an email, the anger intensifies; the words, unaccompanied by softening body language or tone of voice, become weapons as sharp as any sword and as explosive as dynamite. As a diocesan bishop, I often saw church conflicts over minor matters ratchet up beyond my ability to reconcile. Imagine the following scenario: An unhappy parishioner writes an email complaining about the new wall paint in the parish hall. It's a trivial matter, to be sure, but the parishioner sends the angry email to five others, who themselves get caught up in the anger and forward the email to even more people. By the time the priest finds out, let alone the bishop, the whole parish is up in arms. What began as a small matter of "food and drink" has now become a shouting match, people accusing one another of poor taste, bad faith, and arbitrary decision-making. It is not unlikely that people will leave that parish forever if they come out on the losing side of the conflict. How I wish I were exaggerating!

In early 2014, two parallel, internet-based conflicts erupted in the Episcopal Church. One of the church's more traditional seminaries invited a progressive bishop to visit the seminary and to preach, a good-faith effort on the seminary's part to reach out and build bridges. The response, however, was explosive. The traditional blogosphere erupted in anger, with harsh accusations that the seminary was selling out its principles. At almost the same time, a progressive diocesan bishop asked his diocese, as part of a Lenten study program, to read a book by Rick Warren, pastor of Saddleback Community Church in California and a well-known and respected leader who is associated with a traditional perspective on many issues. The response was equally explosive. This time, the progressive blogosphere erupted in anger. Many accused the bishop of—you guessed it—selling out his principles. I don't know if many people in the traditional or progressive communities saw the commonalities, but I found it a helpful cautionary tale.[31] "Wrangling over words," Paul warns Timothy, "ruins those who are listening."

That said, Paul goes on to remind Timothy that inappropriate words can, at times, point to deficient faith. "Avoid profane chatter," he says, "for it will lead people into more and more impiety, and their talk will spread like gangrene." Then he gets specific: "Among them are Hymenaeus and Philetus, who have swerved from the truth by claiming that the resurrection has already taken place. They are upsetting the faith of some." We don't know the details of their "profane chatter," but in some way, Hymenaeus and Philetus were misrepresenting the resurrection. Perhaps, as some scholars have speculated, they took Paul's description of baptism in Romans—"we have been buried with [Christ] by baptism into death, so that, just as Christ was raised from the dead by the glory of the Father, so we might walk in newness of life"—as the final word on resurrection. Nothing more is going to happen; resurrection is merely a symbolic stage in a Christian's spiritual development. On the other hand, perhaps, like the Christians in Thessalonica, they had concluded that "the day of the Lord is already here" (2 Thessalonians 2:2), and somehow it has passed them by. Jesus has already raised up everyone he plans to raise, and the rest of us have missed the resurrection boat. Whatever the particulars of Hymenaeus and Philetus's teaching, their words unsettled young Christians and harmed their faith. Paul's criticism is harsh: False teaching is profane, impious, and (in a spectacularly chilling metaphor) gangrenous.

The first century, like the twenty-first, presented a wide assortment of religious options, a "spiritual cafeteria" of ideas and notions, and these notions inevitably made their way almost unconsciously into the early church. Be careful, Paul warns Timothy, not to allow God's people to absorb false ideas that will draw them away from the core message of the gospel. Like our counterparts two thousand years ago, we too can unknowingly absorb ideas and notions—from the internet, from the "spirituality" section at a bookstore, even from Christian media—as destructive as those which Hymenaeus and Philetus proposed.

Sociologists Christian Smith and Melinda Lundquist Denton, studying the spiritual lives of American teenagers, concluded:

> The *de facto* dominant religion among contemporary U. S. teenagers is what we might well call "Moralistic Therapeutic Deism." The creed of this religion, as codified from what emerged from our interviews, sounds something like this:
>
> 1. A God exists who created and orders the world and watches over human life on earth.
>
> 2. God wants people to be good, nice, and fair to each other, as taught in the Bible and by most world religions.
>
> 3. The central goal of life is to be happy and to feel good about oneself.

4. God does not need to be particularly involved in one's life, except when God is needed to resolve a problem.

5. Good people go to heaven when they die.[32]

This religion is a kind of spiritual pastiche, with dabs of Christianity, contemporary culture, and new-age pop psychology mixed together. But it is not, in my experience, limited to teenagers. Many Christians, young and old, are unconscious Moralistic Therapeutic Deists. They do not intentionally deny the faith; rather, they are simply unaware that these ideas are far removed from the heart of the gospel. The ideas sound so reasonable, so fair, so kind. Paul's warning to Timothy is as apt today as it was when he first uttered it. He is not urging doctrinal correctness for its own sake but because it is spiritually urgent. Elsewhere (for example, and most powerfully, in 1 Corinthians 15:3-11) Paul outlines the basics of the Christian faith. Here, as he mentors Timothy in his future role as a defender of the faith, he takes those basics for granted; they undergird both the warning and the positive message that follows. Words, whether the careless words of a knockdown, drag-out church fight or the more insidious words that distort or water down the faith, can wither and destroy the hearers. But well-handled words can also offer life and hope.

Second, Paul says, be confident about words. "Do your best to present yourself to God as one approved by him, a worker who has no need to be ashamed, rightly explaining the word of truth." Later in the letter, Paul will talk about the content of teaching. Here his focus is on process rather than content. "Rightly explaining" translates a Greek word, *orthotomeo*, which has to do with cutting a straight line. When you teach, Paul says, you must be careful to present what the text says, not what you want it to say. Your job is to be as accurate and as clear as you can, using all the tools at your disposal to understand what the text says and then to present it faithfully.

Of course, the phrase "word of truth" does not refer to the Bible as we have it today. When Paul wrote his final letter to Timothy, portions (but not all) of the New Testament had been written, but the New Testament itself had not yet been assembled. Apostolic writings, including material that would be incorporated into the gospels, circulated informally around the churches.[33] The "word of truth" in 2 Timothy probably refers to what we call the Old Testament. Throughout the New Testament, preachers—and Jesus himself—look to the Hebrew Scriptures as the fount of revelation. "Then beginning with Moses and all the prophets, [Jesus] interpreted to [Cleopas and his companion] the things about himself in all the scriptures" (Luke 24:27), we're told in the story of the walk to Emmaus. Later, speaking to an assembly of disciples, Jesus "opened their minds to understand the scriptures" (Luke 24:45). Philip's history-changing encounter with the Ethiopian eunuch centered on an Old Testament text (Isaiah 53:7) and continued with a wide-ranging survey of the Bible: "Then Philip began to speak, and starting with this scripture, he proclaimed to him the good news about Jesus" (Acts 8:35). Both Peter (Acts 2:14-36) and Paul (Acts 13:16-41) preach evangelistic sermons based on the Hebrew Scriptures, and Paul's bullet-point summary of Jesus' death and resurrection (1 Corinthians 15:3-11) reminds his readers twice that the events occurred "in accordance with the scriptures." Timothy's job, then, is to "rightly explain" the scriptures, demonstrate how they point to Jesus, and use them as the springboard to proclaim the gospel.

Workers indeed have "no need to be ashamed" as long as they carry out their craft under agreed limitations. Christian leaders, to begin with, are not free simply to share what's on their mind. While they may have opinions—even correct, spiritually mature opinions—on a variety of matters, the starting point for all Christian teaching is the text of scripture. A sermon or a teaching that's a mere commentary on current events, recent books and movies, or the speaker's emotional or spiritual health fails to meet this important test. The first question a preacher or teacher must ask is, "What does the text say?" Only then can he or she add, "What does the text mean? What does it mean to me and to our world?" It is true, of course, that Christians of goodwill can disagree about the meaning of a text or how it should be applied to our lives. That is why Paul wisely begins this section of his letter by saying, "Do your best." We must approach the work of teaching with humility and the recognition that we can be wrong, sometimes profoundly wrong, as we grapple with the biblical message. Neither Timothy nor we can claim that our understanding of scripture is infallible, but we are to strive to present the text as honestly as we possibly can.

Having done so, we are also free. Preaching and teaching should never be doctrinally idiosyncratic. "The faith that was once for all entrusted to the saints" (Jude 3) is a given, but it is not meant to be rigid. Christian teachers, after all, can look to the example of Jesus himself, who taught in large measure by means of stories with a "bite." Timothy and his successors are free to employ a variety of creative methods to present the faith. We can employ parables, poems, personal testimony; stories from the history of the church and stories from our lives today; visual aids, songs, and the posing of pointed questions. Christian teaching is limitless when it comes to an expanse of ways to make the scriptures real, to apply them to our lives. An essential piece of equipment in the toolbox of all Christian leaders, and particularly of lay leaders, is testimony—telling our own story in the light of scripture, showing the particular way that the Bible's story has intersected with our own. Be faithful to the text, Paul says to his apprentice, and then you can be as winsome and as innovative as the Holy Spirit takes you. That is why, over two thousand years of church history, faithful preachers and teachers look so different: Augustine of Hippo, convert and bishop, preaching daily in his North African cathedral; John Chrysostom, skilled and powerful orator; Francis of Assisi, God's troubadour, inviting Christians to reclaim the simplicity of

Jesus; Thomas Aquinas, systematic and focused; Martin Luther, transformed and freed by the gospel; John Wesley, whose strangely warmed heart touches millions; Billy Graham, urging us to a decision for Christ; Martin Luther King Jr., whose speeches are rich in biblical allusions and whose call for justice flows directly from the scriptural stream. No generation's great preacher looks like another's, yet, at the center, is Jesus Christ and him crucified (1 Corinthians 2:2).

Paul concludes this section of his letter with a word of encouragement. "But God's firm foundation stands, bearing this inscription: 'The Lord knows those who are his,' and, 'Let everyone who calls on the name of the Lord turn away from wickedness'" (2:19, citing Numbers 16:5 and 16:26). Numbers 16 tells the dramatic story of rebellion in the desert. Korah, Dathan, and Abiram say to Moses, in effect: "What makes you think you're so special?" Moses might be tempted to despair. He has done so much for these people, leading them out of bondage into freedom, and now they reject him. Instead, Moses simply affirms God's sovereignty, and God, in turn, executes judgment: The ground opens up and swallows the rebellious Israelites, and a blast of divine fire consumes the remaining malcontents (Numbers 16:31-35). Remember Israel's past, Timothy, and take heart, Paul concludes. "The Lord knows those who are his."

Paul is reminding Timothy that God is indeed in charge. Like Moses, Timothy will face rebels. Men such as Hymenaeus and Philetus will say to Timothy, "What makes you think you're so special?" Leave the result, Paul says, in God's hands. Your job is "to present yourself to God as one approved." When you've done that, you can trust that "God's firm foundation stands." Christian leaders then and now face the temptation of measuring "success" solely in terms of numbers. Whether this is a parish's average Sunday attendance, congregational finances, or the number of likes on a Facebook post, we measure ourselves and come up, in our own eyes or in the world's, lacking. Paul is urging Timothy never to forget that, in the end, it is God who sees our hearts and knows the worth of our deeds. Nothing that we do for God's sake, however small, goes unnoticed. God sees all.

Joyce is the proverbial little old lady—quite literally. She's less than five feet tall with a shock of white hair. When the congregation at her parish stands to sing a hymn, she becomes invisible, surrounded as she is by a crowd of standard-height adults. One day Joyce came to her priest with a request. She had noticed a homeless encampment under a bridge in the downtown section of her city and felt a prompting to do something. "Could I borrow the large coffee maker and a couple of soup tureens?" she asked. Her priest agreed, and a week later, Joyce turned up at the encampment with coffee and soup. Homeless people gathered around Joyce and a few parishioners who had accompanied her to the encampment; soup and coffee were chaotically distributed and gratefully received, and Joyce and her friends gathered up their pots and left. It had been yet another Matthew 25:40 encounter, an unassuming Christian taking the lead and feeding the hungry.[34] The result? We'll never know. Shortly after Joyce and her friends fed the homeless under the bridge, the city intervened and cleared out the encampment. But Paul's reminder to Timothy speaks a powerful word: Nothing that we do for God's sake, however small, goes unnoticed. God sees all.

My forty-ninth birthday was perhaps my most traumatic. By that time, I had been a priest for nearly a quarter-century. For years I had assumed that if I worked very, very hard, I would live to see the church transformed. I would see the church's numerical decline reversed, I would see the church turn away from theological innovations, I would see the church returned to its former and honored place as a force for good in public life. To that end, I energetically involved myself not only in my parish but also on a diocesan and national level. But on the day that I turned forty-nine, I suddenly realized: it's not going to happen, at least not in my lifetime. Why forty-nine? I'm not sure. Perhaps, just one year shy of fifty, I could no longer claim to be a "young adult." Perhaps I was unconsciously aware that my energies were no longer limitless, that the forces of ecclesiastical inertia were stronger than my physical and spiritual muscle power. Whatever the reason, I was suddenly overwhelmed on my forty-ninth birthday with the knowledge I would pass from the scene with the church still in disarray. It was a devastating moment. Looking back from a distance of more than twenty years, I wish that I had pondered 2 Timothy 2:19 and drawn encouragement from Paul's word to his apprentice. Timothy, after all, was no more assured of success than I was. He, too, would come to the end of his life with tasks undone and a church still in need of repair. And yet, beyond our imagining, God has given Timothy, and us, a role in the building of the kingdom of God.

By definition, all of us—young and old, lay and clergy—play only a small part on a stage much larger than we can see. Like Timothy, we are to use our words, indeed all of our gifts, "as one approved by God…God's firm foundation stands."

QUESTIONS FOR REFLECTION

1. Paul warns Timothy to avoid wrangling over words. Can you think of a time when you were caught up in conflict over something inessential or unimportant? Were you able to recognize what was happening and extract yourself from the conflict?

2. How do you discern when the wrangling is over something important? What are the signs that the issue is one that requires vigorous engagement?

3. As you think about sharing the Christian faith with another person, how do you distinguish between central Christian teaching and your own opinions about political or cultural issues?

4. Which spiritual tasks in your life are still incomplete and likely to remain so? How do you deal with the painful reality that we do not reach perfection this side of the grave? What gives you hope?

Chapter Seven

The Leader's Heart

In a large house there are utensils not only of gold and silver but also of wood and clay, some for special use, some for ordinary. All who cleanse themselves of the things I have mentioned will become special utensils, dedicated and useful to the owner of the house, ready for every good work.

Shun youthful passions and pursue righteousness, faith, love, and peace, along with those who call on the Lord from a pure heart. Have nothing to do with stupid and senseless controversies; you know that they breed quarrels. And the Lord's servant must not be quarrelsome but kindly to everyone, an apt teacher, patient, correcting opponents with gentleness. God may perhaps grant that they will repent and come to know the truth, and that they may escape from the snare of the devil, having been held captive by him to do his will.

—2 Timothy 2:20-26

"So how did you end up at All Saints?" I asked Carla. She and her family had begun worshiping with us at All Saints, Bakersfield, a few weeks earlier, only a couple of years after my arrival as rector in the fall of 1986. "It's a long story," she told me. "When I was a child, my parents and brothers and sisters and I attended a parish in

Orange County. But in the mid-70s, things went wrong." "What?" I asked. "Well," Carla responded, "a wonderful old man served there as priest for many years. We just loved him, and he loved us. He wasn't much of a preacher, but he cared for his people. Then, it must have been around 1975 when I was in junior high school, he hit the mandatory retirement age and had to step down. The bishop sent a young priest in his place." Carla sighed and went on. "I don't remember much about this young priest, can't recall his name or his face, but my parents couldn't stand him. He was brash, self-absorbed, an incessant talker. Finally, after about three weeks, my parents had had it. We dropped out of church and haven't been back since. But now I'm a parent myself, and my family has moved to Bakersfield, and I thought I'd try out All Saints."

As Carla told her story, I felt a stomach-wrenching dread. "Tell me," I asked, fearing the reply, "what was the name of the parish in Orange County?" "St. Joseph's, in Buena Park," Carla answered. It turned out that I was the brash, self-absorbed, talkative young priest who had driven her parents out of church.

Paul turns Timothy's attention to relationships and the critical role they play in leading the Christian community. While Timothy must be careful about how he—and others—use words, it is equally important to put a high priority on what today we call "people skills." Christian leaders, whether lay or ordained, have an enormous responsibility. People will make decisions about the church, and about Jesus himself, based on what they see in the church's leaders. This may not be fair, but it is reality. Who we are speaks more loudly than what we say. How we care for others is the ultimate test of the authenticity of our faith. "I give you a new commandment," Jesus said, "that you love one another...By this everyone will know that you are my disciples, if you have love for one another" (John 13:34-35). Jesus invites the world beyond the church to judge the church on the basis of its relationships. Leading the flock means caring for people, and caring for people means that leaders must attend to their own hearts. What kind of person does the leader need to be? How can we turn our hearts to the task of loving the people for whom Jesus died? Paul has three pieces of pastoral advice for Timothy.

First, know the church. Paul suddenly switches to a surprising metaphor. "In a large house," he tells Timothy, "there are utensils not only of gold and silver, but also of wood and clay, some for special use, some for ordinary. All who cleanse themselves of the things I have mentioned will become special utensils, dedicated and useful to the owner of the house, ready for every good work." While the utensils in a first-century home might be more primitive than the ones we use in the twenty-first, the principle is clear. Our kitchens contain a wide variety of items, from the most precious to the most prosaic: heirloom china and silver; ordinary, daily-use kitchenware; cleaning supplies and scrub brushes. Paul even mentions the less savory items: "ordinary" translates *atimia*, which can also mean "dishonorable." In earlier times, these might include what our forebears called chamber pots; today, we speak of restrooms. The point is that every home hosts a tremendous assortment of contents. Some we treasure, some we simply use, and some we tolerate.

Paul uses this picture to describe the church. The Christian community, after all, is a ragtag collection of people. Yes, a few are saints, people through whom Jesus shines in an unusually spectacular way: utensils of gold and silver, so to speak. Others are vessels of wood and clay, standard brand and rather ordinary Christians. We live lives that sometimes honor the Lord we claim to follow, and sometimes—perhaps often—we do not. Still others shine only dimly and occasionally with the light of Christ, our commitment fragile and our grasp of the faith weak, the most ordinary or even dishonorable of utensils in God's kitchen. The church is not now, and never has been, uniformly committed to the One who cleanses us with his blood and fills us with the Holy Spirit.

We have always been, from the moment of the church's inception, a mixed community in which holiness and sin compete, cooperate, and tragically mingle.

The Christian leader, Paul urges Timothy, must have a realistic understanding of the church in all its glory and all its failure. In the Nicene Creed, we confess "one holy catholic and apostolic Church."[35] The Catechism in *The Book of Common Prayer* goes on to say that the church's catholicity means that "it proclaims the whole Faith to all people, to the end of time."[36] The operative word is "all," which refers not only to the "great multitude that no one could count, from every nation, from all tribes and peoples and languages" (Revelation 7:9) but also to the wondrous variety of people within the church: the super-spiritual and the superficially religious; the ardent and the cynical; the unwilling spouse dragged to church and the prayer warrior who carries the needs of the community in her heart. Every expression of the church, from a globe-spanning ecclesial body to the smallest and most fragile congregation, includes "utensils not only of gold and silver but also of wood and clay, some for special use, some for ordinary." As Screwtape counsels Wormwood,

> One of our great allies at present is the Church itself. Do not misunderstand me. I do not mean the Church as we see her spread out through all time and space and rooted in eternity, terrible as an army with banners. That, I confess, is a spectacle which makes our boldest tempters uneasy. But fortunately it is quite invisible to these humans. All your patient sees is the half-finished, sham Gothic erection on the new building estate. When he goes inside, he sees the local grocer with rather an oily expression on his face, bustling up to offer him one shiny little book containing a liturgy which neither of them understands, and one shabby book containing corrupt texts of a number of religious lyrics, mostly bad, and in very small print. When he gets to his pew and looks around him he sees just that selection

of his neighbours whom he has hitherto avoided. You want to lean pretty heavily on those neighbours. Make his mind flit to and fro between an expression like "the body of Christ" and the actual faces in the next pew. It matters very little, of course, what kind of people that next pew really contains. You may know one of them to be a great warrior on the Enemy's side.[37]

Timothy, Paul says, you must expect the church sometimes to encourage you, often to disappoint you, and always to surprise you. The most unassuming parishioner might turn out to be a spiritual giant. My friend Joy, for example, used to sit in the back of the church building. I noticed that she never opened a prayer book or hymnal. Instead, throughout Holy Eucharist, she would simply look from side to side, back and forth, paying little attention to the action at the front. One day, my curiosity got the better of me, and I asked Joy, "What in heaven's name are you doing?" "Why, I'm praying, Father Ed," she told me. "I look around the pews, and I think about people's needs, and I pray that the service will bless them and give them exactly what they need." Joy was "a great warrior on the Enemy's side," just the kind of quiet, unnoticed Christian whom Screwtape dreaded. Joy's prayers, and those of thousands like her, uphold the church. Christian leaders, Paul tells Timothy, must look at the community in a clear-eyed and realistic way. They must see and celebrate the Joys—and recognize, as well, brothers and sisters who have wandered into danger. The Christian community includes a wondrous variety of utensils.

Second, know yourself. "Shun youthful passions and pursue righteousness, faith, love, and peace, along with those who call on the Lord with a pure heart" (2:22). Paul reminds Timothy to be aware of the dark side of his own nature as well as the God-affirming side. The passions (the King James Version translates *epithumia* as "lusts") that Timothy must avoid are more than the sins of the flesh, be they sexual, gluttonous, or financial. *Epithumia* is "anxious self-seeking,"[38] an obsession with yourself: your dignity, your "perks," even your righteousness. Christian leaders—and especially young Christian leaders, as I remember from painful and embarrassing experience—can be so convinced that they are right that their message and even their presence becomes toxic. Carla's parents certainly saw this clearly in that self-absorbed young priest! The problem, of course, is that Christians are rarely aware of their own character flaws and how those flaws distress others.

C. S. Lewis talks about this phenomenon in his essay "The Trouble with 'X.'" We all have people in our lives, Lewis says, who cause us to pull out our hair. "X" may be an aunt, a co-worker, a neighbor—someone whose temper, laziness, loud and rasping voice, drunkenness, or bad breath drive us to distraction.

> You know, in fact, that any attempt to talk things over with "X" will shipwreck on the old, fatal flaw in "X's" character. And, you see, looking back, how all the plans you have ever made always have shipwrecked on that fatal flaw—on "X's" incurable jealousy, or laziness, or touchiness, or muddle-headedness, or bossiness, or ill temper, or changeableness….I said that when we see how all our plans shipwreck on the characters of the people we have to deal with, we are "in one way" seeing what it must be like for God…[W]hen He looks into that home or factory or office He sees one more person of the same kind—the one you never do see. I mean, of course, yourself. That is the next great step in wisdom—to realize that you are also just that sort of person. You also have a fatal flaw in your character. All the hopes and plans of others have again and again shipwrecked on your character just as your hopes and plans have shipwrecked on theirs.[39]

That phenomenon, tragically, isn't confined to young Christians. We are all "X," and Paul reminds his apprentice that he must know himself well enough to recognize "X" in his own heart and to shun those "youthful passions." I was, after all, "X" to Carla's parents. Christians, and especially those in leadership, must begin their exploration of humanity's brokenness with a profound awareness that they too "have sinned and fall short of the glory of God" (Romans 3:23).

Only when we acknowledge the reality of sin can we take the next step and "pursue righteousness, faith, love, and peace." Paul now turns Timothy's attention to the kind of transformation that Jesus seeks to create in us. He is drawing on his own earlier teaching on the work of the Spirit, who reproduces in the believer something of the character of Jesus himself. "The fruit of the Spirit is love, joy, peace, patience, kindness, generosity, faithfulness, gentleness, and self-control" (Galatians 5:22-23). We could just as easily, and rightly, say that Jesus is love, joy, peace, etc. Our eternal destiny—a destiny foreshadowed during our earthly pilgrimage—is to see "the glory of the Lord, as though reflected in mirror...[and to be] transformed into the same image from one degree of glory to another; for this comes from the Lord, the Spirit" (2 Corinthians 3:18). Our transformation will be complete when we are "like him, for we will see him as he is" (1 John 3:2), living embodiments of the fruit of the Spirit. Meanwhile, Paul tells Timothy, your call is to do all that you can to foster in yourself those character traits of Jesus that will empower your ministry and mark it as authentic.

In one brief sentence, Paul outlines for Timothy a lifelong program. It is not a self-improvement course nor is it a series of tips for living a happy and prosperous life. Nor, at this point, is Paul providing Timothy with a list of skills for ministry. Elsewhere in the letter, he speaks about the tasks that Timothy must perform and the gifts and talents necessary to accomplish them. But here, in this section on the leader's heart, Paul has a different focus. Oddly, Paul deepens the saying of Socrates, as reported by Plato in the *Apology*: "The unexamined life is not worth living."[40] All Christians, and not only leaders, must know themselves and deal honestly and openly with their flaws as well as their strengths. Our first priority is the difficult but essential work of shunning and pursuing. Youthful passions beckon; righteousness, faith, love, and peace beckon as well, in the outstretched hand of Jesus. Know the difference, Paul tells Timothy, and let Jesus shape your life.

Second, "dial it down." Yes, conflict is inevitable. It's a question of when, not if. Conflict can involve a core issue of faith, or it can merely be wrangling over words. Whatever the case, conflict is the cost of Christian community and the bread and butter of Christian leadership. The burden for maintaining order, Paul tells Timothy, falls on the leader.

"Have nothing to do with stupid and senseless controversies; you know that they breed quarrels. And the Lord's servant must not be quarrelsome but kindly to everyone, an apt teacher, patient, correcting opponents with gentleness." In other words, the leader's attitude in the midst of conflict is an essential ingredient in the healing of that conflict. Leaders must dial it down, maintain an attitude of calm, avoid demonizing opponents, and use a tone of voice that ameliorates rather than exacerbates the dispute. No easy task! When conflict erupts, the fight-or-flight mechanism is immediately triggered. While some leaders avoid conflict (flight), many jump in enthusiastically (fight), determined to defeat the opponent and correct errors. While Paul never condones false teaching and never excuses the trivial arguments that can plague or divide Christian communities, he is equally clear that leaders themselves must respond calmly, quietly, and hopefully. The leader's goal, after all, is not to enjoy a good fight but to encourage repentance and deeper faith.

Rabbi Edwin Friedman, who wrote extensively about congregational conflict, argues that the leader's attitude will determine whether the conflict spins out of control or finds resolution. As Tod Bolsinger of Fuller Theological Seminary summarizes Friedman's teaching, "Start by acting on conviction, stay connected, stay calm, stay the course."[41] In other words, people in the midst of conflict take their cue from the leader. Yes, leaders may feel anxious and overwhelmed in the face of intractable conflict; that's a natural human reaction. But if leaders take a deep breath, remain composed, and remind people that no matter what, they belong to Jesus, they can set the tone for the community and bring a measure of peace and confidence. On the other hand, if leaders give way to anger or panic, people will inevitably follow their lead. When leaders dial it down and stay calm, the community will follow their example.

Richard Hooker, an English priest who lived in the second half of the sixteenth century, wrote his famous *Laws of Ecclesiastical Polity* in the midst of profound controversy. The Church of England, separated a second time from the Roman Catholic Church, sought to define its essential nature. On the one side, more extreme Protestants demanded an end to any traces of medieval Catholic practice, and on the other, Roman Catholics sought to return the church to papal obedience. Hooker's *Laws* sought a middle way. What's important about his work is not merely the content of his writing, but the manner in which he presented his ideas in the heated atmosphere of ecclesial conflict. The collect for the feast of Richard Hooker captures something of his spirit:

> O God of truth and peace, you raised up your servant
> Richard Hooker in a day of bitter controversy to defend with
> sound reasoning and great charity the catholic and reformed
> religion: Grant that we may maintain that middle way, not as a
> compromise for the sake of peace, but as a comprehension for
> the sake of truth; through Jesus Christ our Lord, who lives and
> reigns with you and the Holy Spirit, one God, for ever and ever.
> *Amen.*[42]

We would do well to model our own behavior on Hooker's, and to avoid rhetoric that inflames conflict beyond repair.

As he encourages Timothy to "dial it down," Paul adds an important footnote. In the end, it is not Paul or Timothy who will correct errors, large or small. "God may perhaps grant that they will repent and come to know the truth." No amount of pastoral pressure or stunningly clever arguments can accomplish that task unless God is at work. It is God who enables those in error to "escape from the snare of the devil." All of this is an important reminder, lest we imagine that the kingdom of God cannot come without our vigorous prosecution. While Christian leaders must never avoid the responsibility of correcting error and working for peace and reconciliation, we must do so modestly. As Paul tells his friends in Corinth, the ministry God gives us is "...a treasure in clay jars, so that it may be made clear that this extraordinary power belongs to God and does not come from us" (2 Corinthians 4:7).

QUESTIONS FOR REFLECTION

1. The church, Paul tells Timothy, is an enormously diverse community. How have you experienced that diversity? What are the challenges and opportunities of living in community with people different from yourself?

2. "The Trouble with 'X'" includes us. How have you encountered your own faults and flaws? What was your reaction when you discovered how others perceive you?

3. What concrete steps can you take to "pursue righteousness, faith, love, and peace"? What spiritual resources help you as you seek transformation?

4. Paul urges Timothy to "dial it down" in the midst of conflict. How do you remain calm when emotions run high and people are strongly polarized? How do you find the balance between vigorous action to foster reconciliation and trusting God to change people's hearts?

CHAPTER EIGHT

The Leader's World

You must understand this, that in the last days distressing times will come. For people will be lovers of themselves, lovers of money, boasters, arrogant, abusive, disobedient to their parents, ungrateful, unholy, inhuman, implacable, slanderers, profligates, brutes, haters of good, treacherous, reckless, swollen with conceit, lovers of pleasure rather than lovers of God, holding to the outward form of godliness but denying its power. Avoid them! For among them are those who make their way into households and captivate silly women, overwhelmed by their sins and swayed by all kinds of desires, who are always being instructed and can never arrive at a knowledge of the truth. As Jannes and Jambres opposed Moses, so these people, of corrupt mind and counterfeit faith, also oppose the truth. But they will not make much progress, because, as in the case of those two men, their folly will become plain to everyone.

Now you have observed my teaching, my conduct, my aim in life, my faith, my patience, my love, my steadfastness, my persecutions and suffering the things that happened to me in Antioch, Iconium, and Lystra. What persecutions I endured! Yet the Lord rescued me from all of them. Indeed, all who want to live a godly life in Christ Jesus will be persecuted. But wicked people and impostors will go from bad to worse, deceiving others and being deceived.

—2 Timothy 3:1-13

In biblical times, shepherding was a dangerous business. The young David tells King Saul, "Your servant used to keep sheep for his father; and whenever a lion or a bear came, and took a lamb from the flock, I went after it and struck it down, rescuing the lamb from its mouth; and if it turned against me, I would catch it by the jaw, strike it down, and kill it" (1 Samuel 17:34-35). Today's shepherds may not face lions or bears, but their job remains the same: to protect the flock from danger.

For many years I watched shepherds in action—Basque shepherds, whose ancestors had migrated from Spain to Kern County, California, in the nineteenth century, and who continue to tend sheep in the hills around Bakersfield. In the winter, these shepherds would often bring their flocks into town and graze them on vacant lots. I always knew when sheep were near because of the enormous pillars of dust they would kick up. These shepherds lived not in caves like in Bethlehem but in campers, and the most pressing danger was not from predators but from vehicles. Sheep tend to wander, and the shepherds must be ever vigilant, lest the sheep find themselves unwittingly in the path of cars and trucks. Yet the principle remains the same. Shepherds, ancient and modern, protect the sheep from external threats. Jesus himself uses the shepherding image to describe his care for us, his flock. "I am the good shepherd. The good shepherd lays down his life for the sheep. The hired hand, who is not the shepherd and does not own the sheep, sees the wolf coming and leaves the sheep and runs away—and the wolf snatches them and scatters them" (John 10:11-12). Real shepherds interpose themselves between the sheep and the perils that surround them, even at the cost of their own lives. Shepherds must understand the threats that endanger the sheep and take action to protect the flock committed to their care.

Christian leaders, Paul tells Timothy, must be equally vigilant. "You must understand this, that in the last days distressing times will come." As he continues to instruct Timothy on the overwhelming burdens his apprentice will soon undertake, Paul stresses the leader's role as protector of his people. These are hard times, he says. The culture that surrounds you threatens the flock. In these "last days"—the time inaugurated by the resurrection of Jesus—life will get harder, not easier. The world will become an increasingly unfriendly place for followers of Jesus. Dangers, some subtle and some overt, lurk everywhere. We cannot escape them, Paul reminds Timothy, but your task is to recognize the dangers, call attention to them, and take measures to instruct your people on how to live in the midst of a world that can draw you away from Jesus. What strategies does Paul offer as Timothy prepares to guide the church through perilous waters in the coming decades?

First, Paul says, understand the dangers. "For people will be lovers of themselves, lovers of money, boasters, arrogant, abusive, disobedient to their parents, ungrateful, unholy, inhuman, brutes, haters of good, treacherous, reckless, swollen with conceit, lovers of pleasure rather than lovers of God, holding to the outward form of godliness but denying its power. Avoid them!"

Paul knows his culture and is well aware of its dark side. In many ways, this distressing laundry list of negative qualities derives from its first item—"lovers of themselves." The original Greek text of the New Testament did not include punctuation marks or even space between words. Translators and textual scholars supply those marks and spaces, using a combination of context and common sense to determine what fits where. My theory is that we should place a colon after "lovers of themselves," since all of the qualities that follow derive from the primordial human sin: to place ourselves at the center of our own universe and everything else at the periphery. From the dawn of time, Genesis tells us, human beings have said no to God. "Did God say, 'You shall not eat from any tree in the garden'?" Satan asks Eve (Genesis 3:1). Her decision, and Adam's, to disobey God is repeated over and over and over, down the millennia and into our own lives. "Lovers of themselves" is the disease; the rest of the list is a grim array of symptoms.

Is Paul talking about Christians or about the world beyond the church? Perhaps a little of both. Our feet, after all, are awkwardly planted in two worlds. Christians are just as liable to be "lovers of themselves," with all of the malignant behaviors that stem from that disease, as the world that surrounds us. We can become "little tin gods," as J. B. Phillips so aptly puts it in his translation of 1 Peter 5:3,[43] and we join the world in relegating God to the margins. Still, Paul is inviting Timothy to cast a discerning eye on the culture that surrounds the Christian community and to recognize the myriad ways that Christians can be drawn away from wholehearted devotion to Jesus. "Avoid them!" he says.

That command is harder than it seems. More than a decade earlier, in his first letter to the Corinthians, Paul reminds his readers how difficult it is for Christians to completely isolate themselves from the non-Christian world. "I wrote to you in my letter not to associate with sexually immoral persons—not at all meaning the immoral of this world, or the greedy and robbers, or idolaters, since you would then need to go out of the world" (1 Corinthians 5:9-10). In fact, there's always the danger of adopting an attitude of censoriousness, taking pleasure in the world's sins and taking equal pleasure in condemning those sins. Spiritual writer Martin Thornton points out, "Lord Melbourne's notorious remark, 'Things have come to a pretty pass when religion is allowed to invade the sphere of private life,' rightly interpreted, contains more solid sense than is sometimes supposed."[44] While Lord Melbourne, a nineteenth-century British prime minister, doubtless yearned for a religion safely distant from his day-to-day life, there's truth buried in his urbane dismissal. Christian busybodies, lay or ordained, do not further the gospel's cause when they harp on the world's misdeeds. On the whole, it's spiritually safer to focus on our own sins rather than those of people beyond the church. As the psalmist says, "I know my transgressions, and my sin is ever before me" (Psalm 51:3).

Still, the world is a dangerous place, and Paul warns Timothy always to be aware of its power to lure Christians into disobedience. Paul offers two back-to-back examples. "For among them are those who make their way into households and captivate silly women, overwhelmed by their sins and swayed by all kinds of desires, who are always being instructed and can never arrive at a knowledge of the truth." While Timothy doubtless understands this reference, we don't. Perhaps Paul is talking about the unprotected widows of 1 Timothy 5:9-16, women disconnected from their families and, in the setting of a patriarchal society, cast adrift and vulnerable. Whatever's going on, the picture here is one of cultural invasion. These anonymous women have uncritically opened the door to the world, and the world, in its turn, has led them away into a distorted version of the gospel.

Paul's second example, while not anonymous, is equally puzzling. "As Jannes and Jambres opposed Moses, so these people, of corrupt mind and counterfeit faith, also oppose the truth. But they will not make much progress, because, as in the case of those two men, their folly will become plain to everyone" (3:8-9). Who are Jannes and Jambres? These are names that Jewish tradition gives to the magicians who opposed Moses and Aaron and worked counterfeit miracles. "Aaron threw down his staff before Pharaoh and his officials, and it became a snake. Then Pharaoh summoned the wise men and the sorcerers; and they also, the magicians of Egypt, did the same by their secret arts. Each one threw down his staff, and they became snakes; but Aaron's swallowed up theirs" (Exodus 7:10-12). Jannes and Jambres, Paul tells Timothy, offer a dangerous "alternative spirituality" to the real thing. In the same way, he implies, the world can present alluring options in place of the gospel. Christian leaders must be aware of their cultural environment and be ready to shepherd the flock when dangers threaten.

Is the answer, as Rod Dreher argues, a strategic withdrawal from the world, modeled on Saint Benedict's sixth-century community at Monte Cassino?[45] Or is it instead some kind of thoughtful engagement with the culture, aware of its threats but willing to seek mutual understanding and enrichment? Timothy and his successors, down to our own day, have struggled with these questions, and over the centuries the church has moved back and forth between the two models of withdrawal and engagement. Each has its distortions; each can subvert the gospel. If we withdraw entirely from the world, we are no longer the salt and light that Jesus calls us to be (Matthew 5:13-16). On the other hand, if we engage the culture uncritically, we can find ourselves "tossed to and fro and blown about by every wind of doctrine" (Ephesians 4:14). Paul's warning to Timothy—that he understand the dangers and take care to raise a warning hand—places an enormous burden on Christian leaders.

God has given me the gift of two powerful, and contrasting, examples as I ponder these questions: two communities that, in different ways, demonstrate how each answer can be lived with integrity. The first surrounds me as I write these words. I am sitting in the reading room of the Theodore M. Hesburgh Library on the campus of the University of Notre Dame, a great Catholic university with deep Christian roots. When I walk across campus, I hear the bells of the Basilica of the Sacred Heart marking the hours. At the north end of a long greenbelt stands the administration building, topped by its famous Golden Dome and a statue of the Blessed Virgin Mary gazing out at her university. At the same time, Notre Dame opens its gates and its heart to the world. Speakers representing a wide variety of viewpoints regularly appear on campus, often to the dismay of people on both sides of the political spectrum. Among my acquaintances at the university are philosophers, theologians, entomologists, business professors, biblical scholars, Medievalists, Renaissance specialists, and mathematicians. This Christian community engages the world in a wondrous assortment of ways.

About twenty-five miles south and a bit east of where I sit is the second example—the Amish community. A swath of Northern Indiana might be called "Anabaptist Central," and the most conservative representatives of the Anabaptist tradition are the Amish. When I drive through Amish country, I enter a different world. No electrical power lines reach out to Amish farms. I must drive cautiously because I share the road with horse-drawn buggies that amble at their own leisurely pace. The Amish dress simply, send their children to Amish-run schools, and marry within their own communities. They eschew most modern conveniences, though some Amish communities permit the use of cell phones (with the proviso that people charge their phones at the home of an "English"—that is, non-Amish—neighbor). The Amish are not, however, mere antiquarians. What appears quaint and picturesque to us is a serious attempt to respond to Saint Paul's command: "Therefore come out from them, and be separate from them, says the Lord" (2 Corinthians 6:17, quoting Isaiah 52:11). The Amish recognize that the world poses grave dangers and take concrete steps to avoid its entanglements.

Christian leaders must prayerfully guide their flocks through the complex task of responding to the world and its values and claims. Engagement? Withdrawal? Or some more nuanced stance between the poles? Years before, Paul himself seems to employ both strategies during his brief layover in Athens. "While Paul was waiting for [Silas and Timothy] in Athens, he was deeply distressed to see that the city was full of idols" (Acts 17:16). Paul's distress could well have led to a sermon denouncing idolatry and the moral deterioration that accompanies it (as described by Paul in Romans 1:18-25). Instead, in Athens Paul both affirms and subverts the culture. "Athenians," he tells them, "I see how extremely religious you are in every way. For as I went through the city and looked carefully at the objects of your worship, I found among them an altar with the inscription, 'To an unknown god.' What therefore you worship as unknown, this I proclaim to you" (Acts 17:22-23). Paul's sermon affirms the one God as Creator; he even manages to quote pagan poets Aratus, Cleanthes, and Epimenides and find Christian overtones in their writing: "For 'in him we live and move and have our being'; as even some of your own poets have said, 'For we too are his offspring'" (17:28). He ends with a word of judgment and a proclamation of the resurrection (17:31). This sermon, to be sure, is addressed to a pagan rather than a Christian audience, but it is helpful to see Paul both challenging and engaging the world, affirming what he can and rejecting what he must. He clearly understands the culture in which he ministers and engages the culture in a way that both honors the gospel and speaks realistically about the world and its values.

Second, Paul tells Timothy, respond wisely. Wisdom, for Paul, means looking with clear eyes at his own life, at the trials he's faced, at the transformation that the Lord has accomplished in him, and above all at Jesus' faithfulness as he has struggled with adversity. "Now you have observed my teaching, my conduct, my aim in life, my faith, my patience, my love, my steadfastness, my persecutions and suffering the things that happened to me in Antioch, Iconium, and Lystra. What persecutions I endured! Yet the Lord rescued me from all of them." Dealing with a hostile environment, far from embittering Paul, has led him more deeply into the heart of Jesus. He recognizes, above all, that attending to his own spiritual health is the most powerful way to prepare for the adversity that will inevitably come his way.

It can sound as though Paul is bragging to Timothy about his spiritual progress. Yet Paul never forgets—as he so forcefully told Timothy in his previous letter—that he "was formerly a blasphemer, a persecutor, and a man of violence" (1 Timothy 1:13) and that the work of transformation is a process yet to be fully accomplished. "Not that I have already obtained [perfection] or have already reached the goal; but I press on to make it my own, because Christ Jesus has made me his own" (Philippians 3:12). Looking back at his long ministry, Paul can see God's hand in the midst of severe hostility—shaping him, growing in him the fruit of the Spirit, enabling him to endure and even to flourish. Guiding the church as it navigates the complexity of living in a spiritually alien culture, Paul implies, will make you a faithful, patient, loving, and steadfast leader.

But always remember, Paul adds, that it will be hard. "Indeed, all who want to live a godly life in Christ Jesus will be persecuted. But wicked people and impostors will go from bad to worse, deceiving others and being deceived." Adversity, Paul tells Timothy, is inevitable, though the form that adversity takes changes from era to era. In the United States, Christians sometimes claim to be persecuted because it is no longer legal to say the Lord's Prayer in a public school or because nativity scenes cannot be displayed on the courthouse lawn. These could best be described as irritating signs of a secular culture rather than persecution as Paul and his companions experienced it. The real thing does, however, exist on our planet, sometimes in virulent forms. A few years ago, an Anglican Christian in Peshawar, Pakistan, sent me a Facebook friend request. His name was William Gulham. Although we had never met, the Anglican world boasts a remarkably small gene pool; and Facebook has, if nothing else, served as a reminder of how interconnected we are. Anglicans around the world (and, I imagine, Christians in other traditions have the same experience) know more about one another than we did even a few years ago. Though we never met face to face, William and I exchanged a few notes, and I came to admire his commitment to Jesus in an environment both hostile and dangerous. On Sunday, September 22, 2013, two suicide bombers forced their way into All Saints Church, Peshawar, and detonated their explosive vests. One hundred and twenty-seven

Christians died. I remember, later that day, logging onto Facebook to see if William had survived the attack. Tragically, he did not. "All who want to live a godly life in Christ Jesus will be persecuted." Paul's words to Timothy are as true in our own day as they were in his.

Christians in the United States are unlikely to face the deadly hostility that William Gulham experienced and that ultimately claimed his life. But a sense of separation, of not entirely belonging to our culture, is for Christians a "when" rather than an "if." The cultural dissonance we experience may be subtle, a painful realization that we do not share core values with the persons with whom we live, or shop, or work. It may be a sharper disconnection: finding ourselves in a setting where people of faith are looked down upon as less-than-intelligent yokels; sensing pressure to be silent about Jesus and his place in our lives; feeling a kind of internal check about speaking openly about our faith because it's considered socially unacceptable. Perhaps, someday that hostility may morph into something more clearly dangerous. Whatever the case, the test for Christian leaders is not merely how they deal with adversity, opposition, and persecution in their own lives, be it subtle or overt. The real test is how leaders inform, guide, and protect the flock of Christ; how they speak a word of warning without becoming shrill or alarmist; how they equip their people to respond to the world with faith and courage. That is the task that Paul places in the hands of his successor. It is as urgent a task for leaders in our day.

QUESTIONS FOR REFLECTION

1. How have you experienced external dangers to your faith?
    What elements of the culture you live in pull you away from the
    gospel?

2. On the other hand, how do you identify elements of that
    culture that are harmless or even beneficial? Are there times
    when secular culture can enhance the gospel? What strategies
    do you employ to discern the difference?

3. Paul warns Timothy that the world's values produce "lovers
    of self." How have you encountered that phenomenon in your
    own life? What form does it take?

4. Paul's sermon in Athens is a model of cultural engagement
    and challenge. When has God led you to engage and affirm the
    culture? To challenge it?

PART IV

STICK TO THE BASICS

A friend and colleague once told me that he has three rules for effective Christian leadership: 1: Show up. 2: Smile. 3: Don't be a jerk. There's nothing complicated here, nothing subtle. Stick to the basics, my friend says. Build positive relationships and attend to people in a loving way, and you will avoid the disaster that tragically befalls so many leaders who ignore these principles.

Paul has a similarly direct piece of advice for Timothy. His counsel is as forceful and blunt as my friend's, and the advice comes on the heels of Paul's reminder to Timothy that he is a shepherd. He has a flock to care for. He is to use words with thoughtful precision, cultivate a leader's heart, and remain aware of the world in which his flock lives. But now what? Paul's answer echoes Dietrich Bonhoeffer's words, written nearly two millennia later. *"Only he who believes is obedient,"* Bonhoeffer said, *"and only he who is obedient believes."*[46] Paul tells his protégé that his ministry comes down to two primary tasks: know what you believe, and do what you're told. These are two sides of a single coin, the basics of Christian leadership.

Sticking to these basics, however, is harder than it sounds. Most Christians tend to gravitate around one pole or the other. For some, believing comes naturally. Scripture, prayer, study, and the contemplative life give energy and focus. It is no surprise that

Trappist monk Thomas Merton, nearly fifty years after his death, continues to inspire generations of Christians who yearn to know, pray, and believe more deeply. Other Christians are wired for action. Whether the action is advocating for social justice, feeding the hungry, or going door to door on an evangelistic crusade, some Christians prefer to do something. They want to make a difference, and making a difference requires action. Leaders as diverse as William Wilberforce, Martin Luther King Jr., and Billy Graham serve as models for action-oriented Christians.

Paul tells Timothy that his life and ministry must incorporate both poles: faith and action, belief and obedience, going deeper and working harder. In other words, Paul reminds Timothy that before assuming the mantle of leadership, he must structure his life to know and understand "the mystery that has been hidden throughout the ages and generations and has now been revealed to his saints...Christ in you, the hope of glory" (Colossians 1:26-27). Remember what you believe, Timothy, and daily plunge the depths of your faith. At the same time, Paul urges Timothy to structure his life around the great task of proclaiming and embodying the gospel. "We are ambassadors for Christ," Paul has earlier told his friends in Corinth, "since God is making his appeal through us" (2 Corinthians 5:20). Ambassadors must dedicate themselves to representing the king, and the king we serve is the King of kings and Lord of lords. Serving Jesus, not least as a leader in the church, is exhausting work, and that work is now Timothy's. And so Paul lingers over the two basics of Christian leadership. He asks Timothy once more to ponder the heart of the faith and how he came to believe it. He asks him, in almost the same breath, to recall the specific ways that Jesus invites him to live that faith with courage and integrity.

CHAPTER NINE

Know What You Believe

But as for you, continue in what you have learned and firmly believed, knowing from whom you learned it, and how from childhood you have known the sacred writings that are able to instruct you for salvation through faith in Christ Jesus. All scripture is inspired by God and is useful for teaching, for reproof, for correction, and for training in righteousness, so that everyone who belongs to God may be proficient, equipped for every good work.

—2 Timothy 3:14-17

Because I was raised in a secular home, my childhood memories of church are sparse. Only once in my growing-up years did I attend Sunday School, almost off-handedly: a friend asked me to join him one Sunday morning, and I reluctantly agreed. The experience was uninspiring. The lesson, I recall, centered on good seed and bad seed. Although I don't remember the biblical basis for the lesson, I suspect that Matthew 13:24-30, the Parable of the Weeds, carried the scriptural freight. The teacher asked, "What kind of seed are you?" I came away from that Methodist Sunday School classroom feeling unsettled, a little guilty, and convinced that this was not only my first Sunday School class but also my last. After all, I concluded,

I was probably an example of a bad seed. I wasn't sure if the Bible was scary or merely silly, but in either case, I wanted nothing to do with it.

Timothy's youthful experience is considerably more positive! We've already seen that his grandmother Lois and mother, Eunice, had an enormous impact on Timothy's spiritual development. The faith of these two godly women have energized his own. Now Paul fleshes out the picture with a reminder of how Lois and Eunice have commended the faith to him. "But as for you, " Paul tells Timothy, "continue in what you have learned and firmly believed, knowing from whom you learned it, and how from childhood you have known the sacred writings that are able to instruct you for salvation through faith in Christ Jesus."

In other words, Timothy was brought up with the scriptures, which in Paul's day meant the writings that Christians call the Old Testament. Much, however, is left unsaid. We're not told the details of Timothy's scriptural education. In the New Testament era, and for 1,500 years afterward, people didn't have copies of the Bible in their homes. That awaited the invention of moveable type. Most people simply heard the scriptures read aloud from enormous scrolls in the synagogue and later in the church. Jesus unrolling the scroll in the synagogue in Nazareth (Luke 4:16-17) gives us an idea of how cumbersome that process actually was. Did Lois and Eunice follow up with instruction at home? If so, how did they do that? Did they systematically discuss the biblical passage that had been read in the synagogue earlier that day? Or was their teaching more spontaneous? Paul doesn't tell us. We can infer that Timothy's biblical education began even before the conversion of Lois and Eunice to the Christian faith, which probably occurred during Paul's visit to Lystra and Derbe, toward the end of his first missionary journey (Acts 14:8-20). Later, Lois and Eunice discover that the Hebrew Scriptures point to Jesus, and their biblical mentoring takes on a new and Christ-centered focus. Elsewhere,

Paul talks about Christ being formed in Christians (Galatians 4:19). A central part of that formation, for Timothy and for us, is biblical. As the scriptures find a home in our hearts and minds, we come to know Jesus and to discover his purpose for our lives. The scriptures, Paul says, "instruct you for salvation." The Greek verb is *sophizo*, whose root is *sophia*, wisdom. God imparts wisdom to us through the sacred writings that draw us to Jesus.

Paul goes on to remind Timothy about two distinctive qualities of scripture, qualities that make these writings unlike any other. First, he says, the Bible is infused with God's life: "All scripture is inspired by God." Here Paul is using an unusual compound Greek word: *theopneustos*, which links two words: *theos* (God) and *pneuma* (Spirit). But *pneuma*, like its Hebrew equivalent *ruach*, can also be translated as "wind" or "breath." And so "inspired by God" does not fully capture the depth of what Paul is telling Timothy. The New International Version renders the passage: "All scripture is God-breathed." God has breathed into these human words in a way that hearkens back to the story of creation. "The Lord God formed man from the dust of the ground, and breathed into his nostrils the breath of life; and the man became a living being" (Genesis 2:7). Just as human beings are unique in the created order—bearing as they do the divine "spark" and image (Genesis 1:26)—so the scriptures are unique among writings. It is true, of course, that poetry can ennoble us, history can challenge us, philosophy can stretch us, and fiction can deepen our understanding of human nature. My own life is enriched daily by the books I read. But the Bible, Paul insists, is different. As no other book can do, the scriptures unveil the heart of God; they give us glimpses of the One who called creation into existence, singled out a people for his own possession, sent his Son to live, die, and rise for us, and wondrously invites us to share in the building of his kingdom.

The passage does not, however, give us a detailed theory of biblical inspiration—of how, precisely, God interacted with the Bible's human authors and enabled their words to become the vehicle for his Word. Christians have been reflecting on 2 Timothy 3:16 since Paul wrote those words, and even after two millennia have no common understanding of what it means to call the Bible "inspired" or "God-breathed." Was God's message dictated verbatim to the biblical authors so that their primary work was simply to function as scribes? Or was the process of inspiration, from the authors' perspective, less clearly directive? Perhaps, as they wrote a wide range of literature, from narrative to poetry to law codes to letters to visions to a broad category often called "wisdom," they were unaware of the Spirit's subtle nudges. They didn't need to be. Later, the Jewish community for the Hebrew Scriptures, and the Christian Church for both testaments, would recognize the documents' authority, the normative nature of these writings, and declare them canonical. *The Book of Common Prayer*, with characteristic modesty, says: "We call Holy Scriptures the Word of God because God inspired their human authors and because God still speaks to us through the Bible."[47] We may not know the "how" of biblical inspiration, but with Paul, we can affirm the fact of it. God has put himself in a unique way into these ancient words and bids us to listen and obey.

"All scripture is inspired by God." These five words do not provide us with detailed instructions on how we are to understand the scriptures and apply them to our lives. If, as the prayer book says, God speaks to us through the sacred writings, we need extra-biblical help to know how to listen! Once more, the prayer book offers guidance, this time in the form of a collect (a formal prayer that summarizes or "collects" the theme of a particular Sunday):

> Blessed Lord, who caused all holy Scriptures to be written for our learning: Grant us so to hear them, read, mark, learn, and inwardly digest them, that we may embrace and ever hold fast the blessed hope of everlasting life, which you have given us in our Savior Jesus Christ; who lives and reigns with you and the Holy Spirit, one God, for ever and ever. *Amen.*[48]

This prayer, composed by Archbishop Thomas Cranmer for the first *Book of Common Prayer* in 1549 and revised only slightly in later editions, reminds us that understanding the Bible is a process rather than a single event. Each verb takes us more deeply into the journey of applying the Bible's message to our lives. We are to hear the scriptures (paying attention as they're read aloud); read them (there is no substitute for actually picking up the Bible and reading it); mark what we read (lingering on the words, asking what the words are saying and what they mean); learn the contents (memorizing scripture is a wonderful way to plant the Bible in our hearts and minds); and finally inwardly digest the Bible (pondering the biblical message, returning again and again to passages that nourish us, challenge us, encourage us). Karl Barth speaks of "the strange new world of the Bible."[49] For Timothy and for us, coming to grips with that world, allowing it to take root in our hearts and minds, is a lifelong program.

The program, however, has a purpose, and that brings us to Paul's second point. God uses the scriptures, he tells Timothy, to transform our lives. Not only is scripture inspired, not only has God breathed life into these human words, but also it is "useful for teaching, for reproof, for correction, and for training in righteousness, so that everyone who belongs to God may be proficient, equipped for every good work." The Bible reveals God's plan to restore all creation to himself—and more: The Bible guides and directs us, gives shape to our lives, and enables us to live according to God's purposes for us.

To begin with, the Bible is useful for teaching. It is true that "the heavens are telling the glory of God; and the firmament proclaims his handiwork" (Psalm 19:1). It is true as well that "ever since the creation of the world [God's] eternal power and divine nature, invisible though they are, have been understood and seen through the things he has made" (Romans 1:20). But the story—Creation and Fall, the call of Abraham, the rescue of Israel from slavery in

Egypt, the revelation on Mount Sinai, the conquest of the Promised Land and the ups and downs of Israel's history in the centuries that followed, the warnings and pleas of the prophets, and above all the life, death, and resurrection of Jesus and his promise that in "the fullness of time" God will "gather up all things in [Christ], things in heaven and things on earth" (Ephesians 1:10)—is found solely in the Bible. There alone does God show us who he is, what he has done, and how the story will finally end, when "the kingdom of the world [becomes] the kingdom of our Lord and of his Messiah, and he will reign forever and ever" (Revelation 11:15). The Bible teaches us the big picture, centered on Jesus Christ and drawing us at last into "the Great Story which no one on earth has read: which goes on for ever: in which every chapter is better than the one before."[50]

More than that, Paul tells Timothy that scripture is useful for reproof and correction. The Bible shows us where we've gone wrong and how to redirect our lives. That was certainly my own experience. In fact, it's how I became a Christian believer. I mentioned at the beginning of this chapter and elsewhere in the book that my upbringing was entirely secular. My first religious experience came at the age of fifteen when I decided that I did not believe in God. My conversion to atheism was, if anything, more dramatic than my conversion to Christianity some years later. I can remember where I was standing, in the downstairs room of my family's home in Connecticut, when I said to myself, "There is no God." I had fallen under the spell of novelist, philosopher, and atheist Ayn Rand, whose book *Atlas Shrugged* systematically laid out an Objectivist philosophy that rejected any notion of the divine. My atheism was energetically evangelical: I did my best (though happily did not succeed) to convince my friends that God does not exist. Armed with *Atlas Shrugged* and filled with a convert's zeal, I went off to college ready to face the world.

And it was there, in a two-semester Bible as Literature class at the University of Southern California, that I came face to face with

Jesus Christ. At the time, taking the class seemed almost accidental. My declared major was ancient history, and I hoped that someday I might earn a Ph.D. and teach on the college level. Because biblical history intersects with the history of the ancient Egyptians, Assyrians, Babylonians, Hittites, Persians, Greeks, and Romans, I decided that I ought to have at least a passing acquaintance with the literature of the Bible. And so, on a lark, I signed up for Dr. Gerald A. Larue's course.

Dr. Larue was famous across campus as an entertaining lecturer, a skeptic with a twinkle in his eye and a warm smile on his face— and a brilliant scholar. Once a minister of the United Church of Canada, he had lost his faith and came to USC to teach, of all things, the Bible.[51] He held generations of students in his thrall, and I am grateful to have been one of them. Under his tutelage, I learned the broad sweep of the Bible's contents. But in my case, Dr. Larue's skepticism about the scriptures had the opposite of its intended effect. As I read the biblical text for the first time, even in the light of scholarly debunking, something happened. C. S. Lewis, describing the early stages of his own conversion, says: "A young man who wishes to remain a sound Atheist cannot be too careful of his reading. There are traps everywhere—'Bibles laid open, millions of surprises,' as Herbert says, 'fine nets and stratagems.' God is, if I may say it, very unscrupulous."[52] And so, most unscrupulously, the Holy Spirit used Dr. Larue to introduce me to the Bible. Reading assignments included large chunks of scripture, whole books at a time, and I devoured them if not religiously, at least eagerly. This was, I thought, very interesting stuff. Interesting, yes, but as I read, God was quietly but powerfully changing my heart. One day, I recall, I was reading the second half of the Book of Isaiah in preparation for a test and came upon this passage:

> He was despised and rejected by others;
>> a man of suffering and acquainted with infirmity;

and as one from whom others hide their faces
>> he was despised, and we held him of no account...

All we like sheep have gone astray;
>> we have all turned to our own way,

and the Lord has laid on him
>> the iniquity of us all (Isaiah 53:3,6).

I had no idea, of course, that for two millennia Christians have seen in this passage a foreshadowing of the suffering of the Messiah. Yet, on some still inarticulate level, I knew that these words were somehow...well, important.

Later that academic year, in the second of Dr. Larue's courses, I read the New Testament and encountered Jesus Christ. The gospels brought me face to face with One who claimed my allegiance. I remember reading the Sermon on the Mount for the first time and sensing in Jesus' words not simply an ethical code but a demand for obedience and a claim of Lordship. The "coin dropped," however, as I studied for another exam, this one on Paul's first letter to the Corinthians. It was Easter night 1966, and I was reading this letter, making notes for the test, and came upon these words: "Or do you not know that your body is a temple of the Holy Spirit within you, which you have from God, and that you are not your own? For you were bought with a price; therefore glorify God in your body" (1 Corinthians 6:19-20). Well, I said to myself, I guess I'd better shape up. I didn't know, at the time, that I'd been "had." The scriptures are useful, Paul tells Timothy, for reproof and correction, and my Christian conversion is a minor instance of that major truth.

Minor—but far from unique. The Bible itself bears witness to the transforming power of the scriptural text. When Ezra and his companions read aloud the law of Moses to the newly returned exiles in Jerusalem, "the people wept when they heard the words of the law" (Nehemiah 8:9). Throughout the history of the Christian church, the scriptures have served to reprove and correct, to change the course of lives and redirect God's people in often surprising directions. Saint Antony of Egypt, desert father of the third and fourth centuries and, in many ways, the father of monasticism, experienced conversion when the Bible struck a responsive chord in his heart. His biographer, Saint Athanasius, Bishop of Alexandria, records the event:

> He went into the church pondering these things, and just then it happened that the Gospel was being read, and he heard the Lord saying to the rich man, *If you would be perfect, go, sell what you possess and give to the poor, and you will have treasure in heaven* [Matthew 19:21]. It was as if by God's design he held the saints in his recollection, and as if the passage were read on his account. Immediately Antony went out from the Lord's house and gave to the townspeople the possessions he had from his forebears.[53]

Centuries later, another monk—Martin Luther—discovered new freedom and joy in the gospel as he pondered the Letter to the Romans, and still later, John Wesley's life was transformed as he listened to Luther's exposition of the same scripture.

> In the evening I went very unwillingly to a Society in Aldersgate-street, where one was reading Luther's Preface to the Epistle to the Romans. About a quarter before nine, while he was describing the change which God works in the heart through faith in Christ, I felt my heart strangely warmed. I felt I did trust in Christ; Christ alone, for salvation; and an assurance was given me, that He had taken away my sins, even mine, and saved me from the law of sin and death.[54]

More recently, novelist Andrew Klavan speaks of the role of the Bible in his Christian conversion. "I was reading the Gospel of Mark when the sky, as you might say, opened, and my own resistance at last gave way…I saw the empty tomb and I had faith."[55] Paul and Timothy themselves could add their "Amen."

Paul concludes this section with a word on scripture's role in growing Christian disciples. The Bible, he tells Timothy, trains us in righteousness and enables us to be "proficient, equipped for every good work." The Greek words translated as "proficient" and "equipped" are linguistically related (*artios; exartizo*) and together point to moral, spiritual, and ministerial maturity. The more you absorb the Bible and its message, Paul says, the more accurate your moral compass will be, the deeper your prayer life, and the more confident your new role as a leader in the Christian community. The goal, Paul stresses, is for Timothy to be an effective disciple and a faithful follower of Jesus. A high doctrine of scripture—not only its divine inspiration but also its ability to empower Christians—is an essential ingredient of Timothy's faith and of ours. Paul counsels Timothy, and us, to have miraculous expectations of the Bible. Read it. Soak it in. Meet Jesus in its pages. Listen for his voice, obey his summons, follow without fear. Thus God will prepare us for "every good work."

QUESTIONS FOR REFLECTION

1. When did you hear or read the Bible for the first time? Who introduced you to it?

2. Paul reminds Timothy that "all scripture is inspired by God." How have you encountered the unique nature of the Bible? What makes the Bible different from other forms of literature?

3. Karl Barth describes the Bible as a "strange new world." How have you struggled with the enormous distance between the biblical culture and our own?

4. Can you think of a time when the Bible seemed to speak directly to you? When the Bible taught or reproved or corrected you? What impact did that experience have on your life as a disciple of Jesus?

CHAPTER TEN

Do What You're Told

In the presence of God and of Christ Jesus, who is to judge the living and the dead, and in view of his appearing and his kingdom, I solemnly urge you: proclaim the message; be persistent whether the time is favorable or unfavorable; convince, rebuke, and encourage, with the utmost patience in teaching. For the time is coming when people will not put up with sound doctrine, but having itching ears, they will accumulate for themselves teachers to suit their own desires, and will turn away from listening to the truth and wander away to myths. As for you, always be sober, endure suffering, do the work of an evangelist, carry out your ministry fully.

—2 Timothy 4:1-5

"What do we do now?" Bill McKay asks his campaign manager. In the 1972 film *The Candidate*, McKay, played by Robert Redford, challenges long-serving Crocker Jarmon, California's senior senator, who is running for re-election. Over the course of a long, bitter, and often dirty campaign, Bill McKay chips away at Jarmon's apparently insurmountable lead and, to everyone's surprise, wins the election. At the film's end, McKay sits in a daze, cheering supporters swirling around him, unable to understand what has happened and what it means. He senses, intuitively, that his life is about to change irrevocably. Yet for all of the preparation involved in campaigning for office, he is far from ready for the next step. Everything has become real—and overwhelming. Preparation is over. It's time to get to work. And so he asks, "What do we do now?"

Timothy is no Bill McKay, yet the parallel is striking. For years, Timothy has been preparing to assume leadership. Paul has mentored him, taught him by word and example, and allowed him the privilege of accompanying the apostle on his missionary journeys. Timothy has seen both the joys and the excruciating hardships of apostolic ministry. More than that, Paul has reminded Timothy over and over of the raw material that will undergird his ministry of preaching and teaching. The scriptures are uniquely able, Paul says, to prepare him for any challenge he may face. He will be "proficient [and] equipped." God has given Timothy everything he will need for his future ministry. It is hard to imagine a more thorough training course than the years Timothy spent with Paul, years summarized in this final letter. Yet I can't help wondering if Timothy, as he read Paul's words, sat in a daze like Bill McKay. Preparation is over. It's time to get to work. "What do we do now?"

The opening sentences of 2 Timothy 4 offer Paul's final practical words to his young apprentice. Beginning with verse six, Paul will turn to personal matters, but first he stresses one last time that Timothy is about to inherit an enormous responsibility. The stakes are high: the eternal destiny of those for whom Jesus died. It's time for Timothy to set priorities, to decide where to focus his time and energy, to make painful choices about what he will do and what he will lay aside for the sake of the kingdom of God. And so this closing plea is a cry from the heart of an aging apostle. Once more, he urges Timothy to be faithful to the apostolic mantle he will soon inherit and to set his mind and his will on the great task that Jesus has placed in his care. He does this by reminding Timothy of three essential realities.

First, Paul says, remember that time is running out. There's a breathlessness to Paul's words, a sense of urgency that borders on a fevered intensity. Paul is solemn, relentless, and utterly focused: "In the presence of God and of Christ Jesus, who is to judge the living and the dead, and in view of his appearing and his kingdom, I solemnly urge you: proclaim the message; be persistent whether the time is favorable or unfavorable; convince, rebuke, and encourage, with the utmost patience in teaching."

You must never forget, Paul tells Timothy, that you minister under the steady gaze of the Lord. Jesus is watching you. While that reminder is, at first glance, commonplace, the reality is quite different. Christian leaders often live as "practical atheists." What do I mean by that? Most of us begin our day devoutly enough, with prayer and reflection on scripture. I begin each morning with the church's Daily Office, a round of psalms, biblical readings, canticles, and prayers that helps me reflect on God's call and claim the day for God. Once done with the Office, however, it is temptingly easy to slip into an unacknowledged secular mode of living: to go from hour to hour with no conscious thought of Jesus; to live life in a thoroughly prayer-less way; to career through the day, in other words, as though there were no God. Practical atheism is the bane of "professional" Christians—lay and ordained alike—and Paul's warning to Timothy hits home profoundly. Whether our day is spent in a health clinic or a factory, at the office or at home, in a church building or in a school, we must remember that we minister "in the presence of God and of Christ Jesus," who sees us more clearly than we see ourselves.

More than that, the clock is ticking! Many early Christians, Paul among them, expect Jesus to return soon. Christians should order their lives, Paul tells his friends in Corinth, in the awareness that "the appointed time has grown short" (1 Corinthians 7:29). While there is always the danger that Christians will become so obsessed with the end that they lapse into spiritual delusion, we must nonetheless live expectantly. Jesus will return soon. Later, even in the New Testament era, Christians will come to recognize that while Jesus promises to return, he will do so in his own time and his own way—even if that time seems delayed. "With the Lord one day is like a thousand years, and a thousand years are like one day. The Lord is not slow about his promise, as some think of slowness, but is patient with you, not wanting any to perish, but all to come to repentance" (2 Peter 3:8-9). Whether the Lord returns today or in a thousand years, time is running out. Our proclamation is urgent. Jesus will judge both the living and the dead, and we are among them. Some day we will all "appear before the judgment seat of Christ" (2 Corinthians 5:10).

Many years ago, I served on a body called the Standing Commission on Evangelism. Made up of bishops, priests, and laypersons, the commission's task was to produce resolutions for the Episcopal Church's General Convention on the subject of evangelism, itself a novel idea to most Episcopalians. One member of the commission decided to try his hand at a resolution centering on ministry to senior citizens. While I no longer have the text of this proposal, it read something like this: "Resolved, since elderly people will die soon, it is imperative that we commit ourselves to sharing Christ with them before it's too late." (I confess that, even from memory, this is an over-simplified version.) The commission reacted in horror. "This sounds so…so threatening!" some objected. "We can't be dangling death and judgment in front of people who are coming to the end of their lives." Eventually the resolution was watered down to a harmless and uncontroversial affirmation of the importance of ministry to and with senior citizens. I do understand the objections, and the resolution, as presented, did feel rather harsh and threatening. On the other hand, and most painfully, it's true. Paul's insistence that we persist in proclaiming Christ "whether the time is favorable or unfavorable." The Revised Standard Version more vividly translates the phrase, "be urgent in season and out of season," and rests on an important reality: the eternal destiny of men and women is at stake. C. S. Lewis, preaching at the Church of St. Mary the Virgin, Oxford, in the midst of World War II, stresses how momentous is this sense of urgency:

> It is a serious thing to live in a society of possible gods and goddesses, to remember that the dullest and most uninteresting person you talk to may one day be a creature which, if you saw it now, you would be strongly tempted to worship, or else a horror and a corruption such as you now meet, if at all, in a nightmare. All day long we are, in some degree, helping each other to one or other of these destinations...There are no *ordinary* people. You have never talked to a mere mortal. Nations, cultures, arts, civilization—these are mortal, and their life is to ours as the life of a gnat. But it is immortals whom we joke with, work with, marry, snub, and exploit—immortal horrors or everlasting splendours.[56]

But urgency, Paul reminds Timothy, should not lead to desperation. Timothy is to preach and teach "with the utmost patience." The fact that we are urgent "does not mean that we are to be perpetually solemn. We are to play."[57] This is no mere afterthought. Tone of voice is as important as content. The fanatic wins no hearts. Your call, Paul says, is to present Jesus calmly, giving your hearers time to understand, to internalize, and to respond. Christian leaders, if they are to be effective, balance a sense of urgency with a sense of proportion. Nor will any single leader do all the work. "I planted, Apollos watered, but God gave the growth" (1 Corinthians 3:6). As I write these words, I remember Gene, whom I knew as an unpromising teenager in my early days as a youth pastor. Perhaps, during those dreary youth group meetings in which I struggled to make the gospel relevant, a seed was planted. I will never know.

What I do know is that decades later, and quite by accident, I ran into Gene, who had to remind me who he was. Gene is now a deeply committed Christian and the director of a group of homes for people living with dementia. He has dedicated his life to Jesus and to senior citizens. Whether it was I who planted, or someone else, is not important. God gave the growth. And so we are to be urgent, yes, indeed, but urgency with a footnote that points to patience, time, and God's sovereign power: urgent but never desperate.

Second, Paul says, resist novelties. Paul sternly warns Timothy that even within the church, people will be tempted to enhance, or subtract from, or embellish, the gospel. Earlier, Paul had cautioned Timothy about the world and its potentially dangerous impact on believers. But here, his focus is closer to home. Christians can do themselves in, spiritually speaking, when they succumb to the newest theological fad. "For the time is coming when people will not put up with sound doctrine, but having itching ears, they will accumulate for themselves teachers to suit their own desires, and will turn away from listening to the truth and wander away to myths."

Right now, Paul implies, Christians are more or less on the same spiritual page. They confess "one Lord, one faith, one baptism, one God and Father of all" (Ephesians 4:5-6). But that will not always be the case. During your apostolic leadership, Timothy, temptations will set in. This is a critical moment: False teaching can rob the gospel of its power. Confronting novelties—naming them, challenging them, offering a sound and grounded alternative—is a basic task of Christian leadership, and it cannot be put off. The critical time is coming, inevitably so, even if we wish it were not the case. Early in J. R. R. Tolkien's *The Lord of the Rings*, the wizard Gandalf reminds the reluctant hobbit Frodo that Frodo has no control over the time in which he lives. The Dark Lord has re-emerged in Mordor and is in search of the One Ring that, beyond Frodo's imagining, Frodo now possesses. But Frodo can, Gandalf tells him, choose how he will respond:

"I wish it need not have happened in my time," said Frodo. "So do I," said Gandalf, "and so do all who live to see such times. But that is not for them to decide. All we have to decide is what we do with the time that is given us."[58]

"Itching ears" is the colorful way that Paul describes the pastoral reality Timothy will soon face. Christians will embrace novelties for their own sake, novelties that will draw them away from the core of the gospel. While Paul doesn't specify what those novelties are, other New Testament documents make it clear that Christians in the early church did at times "wander away to myths." The letters of John, for example, tell us that some Christians doubted the "fleshly" reality of Jesus. "Every spirit that confesses that Jesus Christ has come in the flesh is from God, and every spirit that does not confess Jesus is not from God" (1 John 4:2-3). Apparently, some were teaching that Jesus only seemed to be human but was instead a kind of ghost, humanlike but not really human. This heresy came to be known as Docetism (from the Greek *dokeo*, "to seem"). It's an appealing heresy—vaguely spiritual, granting Jesus a special status without involving him in the messiness of human life—and in stark contrast to the New Testament's revolutionary claim that "the Word became flesh and lived among us" (John 1:14). Docetism was only the first of countless novelties with which Timothy, and Timothy's successors down to the present day, have had to contend. Apostolic leadership, Paul tells Timothy, is sticking to the "basics."

And the "basics," plain and unadorned, have the power to touch hearts and change lives. For many years, while serving as bishop of Northern Indiana, I had the privilege of regularly visiting Gethsemane Episcopal Church in Marion, Indiana. Marion is an industrial town about an hour south of Fort Wayne. Its manufacturing base is shrinking. Factories have downsized, work has moved overseas, and the town has more and more come to rely on two Christian colleges as major sources of employment: Indiana Wesleyan University in Marion and Taylor University in nearby

Upland. Over the years, an increasing number of IWU and Taylor students and faculty have been worshiping at Gethsemane, to the point that on some Sundays there may be as many as thirty or forty university-connected people in the congregation. In a small parish like Gethsemane, that's an enormous number. Why are these young evangelical Christians attracted to an ordinary, garden-variety Episcopal church? That's a question I regularly posed. What's bringing you here? Why are you choosing to worship in a church with a standardized liturgy, a church that sings traditional hymns? The answer has surprised me. Over and over, students and faculty offered some variety of this testimony:

> I was raised in a huge megachurch, where I met Jesus. I will always be grateful for that church and its leaders and how they introduced me to the Lord. But what I've found here, at Gethsemane, is somehow more solid. Every week I recite the Nicene Creed, along with millions of Christians around the world—and along with Christians through the ages, going back to 325 CE. Every week I hear scripture, every week I pray for the church and the world, every week I receive the Body and Blood of Christ. I know what's coming. It's simple, and it's plain, and it has its roots in the New Testament.

These college students and faculty have grown up in churches that feature rock bands, video screens, strobe lights, and endless variety. They are deeply grateful for their Christian upbringing and for the spiritual hunger that those churches awakened in them. What they're now seeking is to be grounded.

In an era that demands endless novelty, Paul tells Timothy, it is important to be steady, even predictable, and to present Jesus with as few distractions as possible. And when you have done that, he adds, you can put your energy where it needs to be. This is Paul's third essential reality: Get on with the job. "As for you, always be sober, endure suffering, do the work of an evangelist, carry out your ministry fully." Paul has spoken repeatedly throughout 2 Timothy about his protégé's call, the patience and forbearance that his call requires, and the suffering that it will inevitably entail. What's new here is the specific reference to proclaiming the Good News: "Do the work of an evangelist." The Greek word that Paul uses is *euangelistes*, one who announces good tidings. This word appears in Acts 21:8 with reference to Philip, one of the seven servants set apart in Acts 6:1-6 to care for the needy; Philip goes on to have a crucial role in the conversion of a Samaritan village (8:4-8) and of an Ethiopian court official (8:26-40). In his letter to the Ephesians, Paul lists evangelist as one of the ministries that equips God's people for service and builds up the church (Ephesians 4:11-12). In these closing words of advice, Paul narrows and sharpens the scope of Timothy's work. Above all, Paul says, you are to be an evangelist.

Many Christians cringe at the word. Evangelist calls up unpleasant images: of fanatics standing on street corners and shouting at passersby; of high-pressure sales tactics; of forced conversions and emotional manipulation. The images may be even more personal. Aunt Mabel dragged me to church. Uncle Arthur harangued me with Bible stories. My football coach forced the team to kneel and pray before games. When the word "evangelist"—and its cognate, "evangelism"—don't have a negative valence, they still present a set of confusing, contradictory notions. Is evangelism the same thing as church growth? Does it mean taking a stand on controversial social issues and hoping to attract likeminded people? I recall one bishops' meeting in which our speaker urged us to "rebrand" the church for the sake of evangelism. Change the church's image, she said, and you'll make the church more attractive to Millennials. But is that what an evangelist does? It is no wonder that in the Episcopal Church, and in other Christian communities as well, people shy away from evangelism and evangelists. Leave it to the Evangelicals, we're tempted to say. The whole idea sounds either distasteful or vapid; in both cases, we want nothing to do with it. My friend Bishop Sean Rowe of the Diocese of Northwestern

Pennsylvania and the Diocese of Western New York once joked in my presence that our church should have a new tag line:

The Episcopal Church
Outsourcing Evangelism Since 1789

William Temple (1881-1944), Archbishop of Canterbury and a noted theologian, offers a helpful alternative. He wrote a definition of evangelism that, in modified form, has been adopted by the Lambeth Conference—the once-per-decade gathering of all Anglican bishops—and by the General Convention of the Episcopal Church. Evangelism is "the presentation of Jesus Christ, in the power of the Holy Spirit, in such ways that persons may be led to believe in Him as Saviour, and follow Him as Lord within the fellowship of His Church."[59] This definition is as Anglican, one might say, as tea and crumpets. And it puts the focus in exactly the right place: on Jesus. We are to bend heart, mind, and strength to the one goal of presenting Jesus Christ: presenting him in word and deed, in what we say and how we live our lives, so that men and women will come to believe in him and to follow him in company with brothers and sisters. For Paul in this final word to Timothy, and for William Temple, evangelism is not a program. Service as an evangelist is no mere occupation. It is a way of life, a filter or lens through which all activities are measured. Everything that Timothy is called to do—organizing the fledgling church, training new leaders, teaching, correcting error, protecting the church from corrosive influences, wrestling with the inevitable clashes of personality and viewpoint built into the warp and woof of community—must lead people to Jesus.

In these closing instructions, Paul is not simply burdening Timothy with an additional item for his apostolic job description. Given the enormous responsibility that will soon be his, evangelism in a narrow and programmatic sense would be an oppressive task to tack onto his long list of duties. No, something else is going on here. Paul is reminding Timothy, and us, that the church exists for but one purpose. As the Catechism of *The Book of Common Prayer* concisely puts it: "The mission of the Church is to restore all people to unity with God and each other in Christ."[60] The work of an evangelist, as Paul commends it to Timothy, must undergird all of our ministries, inform our priorities, and give shape to even the most prosaic of activities. The final phrase of these final instructions emphasizes the point. "Carry out your ministry fully." The word translated as ministry, *diakonia*, is not a "professional" word. It has to do with humble service, an attitude of heart, waiting on and caring for others. This calling is not about you, Timothy; it's about the people you serve. Are you presenting Jesus to them? Do they see Jesus in you? Are people drawn to him through your ministry? These questions are as pertinent for us in the twenty-first century as they were for Timothy in the first.

QUESTIONS FOR REFLECTION

1. "Practical atheism" is an ongoing danger for all Christians. Are there times when you go through the day without an awareness of God's presence? How do you recognize it and take action to change course?

2. What gives you a sense of urgency in your ministry? How do you find the balance between this urgency and trusting God to work out God's purposes?

3. Paul warns Timothy to beware of "itching ears." What spiritual novelties are particular risks for Christians today? For you? How do we avoid them? What strategies should leaders adopt to expose and challenge them?

4. What does evangelism look like in your setting? How can you evangelize in a way that both "proclaim(s)...the Good News of God in Christ" and "respect(s) the dignity of every human being" (*The Book of Common Prayer*, p. 305)?

PART V

LAST WORDS

"I'm going to miss you, Ed." Those were the last words that Bishop Robert Rusack ever spoke to me. It was the summer of 1986. I had been serving as rector of St. Joseph's Church, Buena Park, California, for eleven years, and had just accepted a call to become rector of All Saints Church, Bakersfield. Priestly moves are never instantaneous, however, and six weeks separated my painful announcement to St. Joseph's and the trek north to Bakersfield. During that odd "in-between" time, Episcopal Renewal Ministries offered its annual conference on the campus of the University of Southern California. Bishop Rusack was to celebrate the opening eucharist, and conference organizers had appointed me to serve as his chaplain. My role was to assist him in the liturgy, help him with his episcopal regalia, and generally make myself useful. When Bishop Rusack arrived at Bovard Auditorium, his appearance shocked me. Formerly a robust, red-faced, and jovial man, he was pale, shaky, and unsteady on his feet. He told me that he was suffering from neuropathy and would need me to help steady him during the liturgy.

The Holy Eucharist was typical of "renewal" liturgies in the 1970s and 1980s: *The Book of Common Prayer* interwoven with medleys of praise songs and spontaneous moments of prayer, many in the congregation raising their arms in praise. From the altar, the assembly looked like a field of wheat waving in the breeze. As he presided at the eucharist, the bishop's voice was strong, but I had to assist him whenever he stood up from the celebrant's chair.

During a quiet moment near the end of the liturgy, Bishop Rusack leaned toward me, put his hand on my arm, and whispered, "I'm going to miss you, Ed." On the surface, there was nothing remarkable about the comment. In moving from Buena Park to Bakersfield, I would be leaving the Diocese of Los Angeles and transferring to the Diocese of San Joaquin and thus no longer under Bishop Rusack's pastoral oversight. In the early years of my ministry in Los Angeles, I had been one of the "young turks" whom Bishop Rusack had encouraged and mentored, and so my move to Bakersfield closed a chapter in his life and in mine. "I will miss you, too, bishop," I responded.

And yet, when he said those words, I found myself thinking: He's going to die. It came into my mind unbidden and unwelcome, a shadow amid a joyful eucharist. But I didn't have time to ponder that grim thought. The eucharist came to a close with the final blessing, and Bishop Rusack quickly made his way to his car. It was the last eucharist he ever celebrated. Three days later, the bishop suffered a massive heart attack and died. Just a week after that eucharist in Bovard Auditorium on the USC campus, I attended Bishop Rusack's Requiem Mass, my last official event as a priest of the Diocese of Los Angeles. Did Bishop Rusack know that he was going to die? I can't answer that question. Sometimes people have a premonition of their death, and sometimes they don't. And yet there was something final in his words, a goodbye that was more than a "See you later!"

The closing paragraphs of 2 Timothy convey that same finality. Paul ends his formal words of advice with the words, "Carry out your ministry fully." He has said what he needed to say and given Timothy a picture of the enormous responsibility he will inherit. Now Paul's focus turns inward. For the rest of the letter, he's thinking out loud: looking at the shape of his life, pondering his future destiny, remembering the people whose lives he has touched, recalling even the painful and broken relationships that will not, at least in this life, be mended. Although he is no longer instructing Timothy on the duties he will soon undertake, Paul invites his apprentice—and us—to listen in as he ponders his life and his death. In many ways, the most important lesson that any Christian can teach is to show us how to die. The Great Litany of *The Book of Common Prayer* asks God to deliver us "from dying suddenly and unprepared."[61] The timing of our death, whether sudden or as the result of a protracted illness, is beyond our control—but preparedness is not. In these final words, Paul gives us the privilege of watching him as he prepares for the end—and the beginning.

CHAPTER ELEVEN

Present, Past, Future

As for me, I am already being poured out as a libation, and the time of my departure has come. I have fought the good fight, I have finished the race, I have kept the faith. From now on there is reserved for me the crown of righteousness, which the Lord, the righteous judge, will give me on that day, and not only to me but also to all who have longed for his appearing.

—2 Timothy 4:6-8

Joseph Cardinal Bernardin showed us how to die. In the summer of 1996, the Roman Catholic Archbishop of Chicago announced that doctors had discovered a recurrence of cancer in the form of five nodules in his liver. The disease was inoperable, and he had less than a year to live. "While I know that, humanly speaking, I will have to deal with difficult moments, I can say in all sincerity that I am at peace," he declared at a news conference. He concluded: "As a person of faith I see death as a friend, as the transition from earthly life to life eternal." *The New York Times* account of Cardinal Bernardin's announcement adds, with a note of surprise, "Today he appeared serene and cheerful as he read a prepared statement and fielded questions, twice asking reporters, 'whatever your religious affiliation,' to pray for him and promising, in turn, to pray for them and their loved ones."[62] Shortly before he died, Cardinal Bernardin wrote the posthumously published *The Gift of Peace*, a reflection on his life and his impending death. The book begins with a handwritten letter to the reader:

> On a very personal note, I invite those who read this book to walk with me the final miles of my life's journey. When we reach the gate, I will have to go in first—that seems to be the rule: one at a time by designation. But know that I will carry each of you in my heart! Ultimately, we will all be together, intimately united with the Lord Jesus whom we love so much.[63]

Paul too shows us how to die. As he writes the closing words of this final letter to Timothy, Paul's gaze shifts from the present moment, when death seems imminent, to the past and his long apostolic ministry, to the future and his eternal destiny: all of this in three sentences of enormous power.

He begins in the present. "As for me, I am already being poured out as a libation, and the time of my departure has come." Paul, the converted Pharisee, is steeped in the Hebrew Scriptures, and here he draws on a biblical image as he ponders his impending death. Moses had commanded the Israelites to pour out a drink offering (described variously as wine or strong drink) as part of their daily worship (Numbers 15:5-10; 28:7). Now Paul will soon pour out his blood—tradition says that he was beheaded during the persecution initiated by Emperor Nero—as a kind of offering. Earlier, writing to the Christian church in Philippi, Paul used the same image: "But even if I am being poured out as a libation over the sacrifice and the offering of your faith, I am glad and rejoice with all of you" (Philippians 2:17). Paul saw his entire ministry, and now his death, as a "libation," a gift that he offers to the Lord with a glad heart. Far from being a bad thing, his death will glorify Jesus. Ungodly people may swing the ax, but the pouring out of his blood is Paul's last "yes" to Jesus, a final offering to the Lord who has been so faithful to him, and who rescued him from himself years ago on the road to Damascus. "I am now rejoicing in my sufferings for your sake," he had told the Christians in Colossae, "and in my flesh I am completing what is lacking in Christ's afflictions for the sake of his body, that is, the church" (Colossians 1:24). Paul's final words in 2 Timothy are of a piece with the way that he has viewed his apostolic ministry: as an offering for the sake of Jesus and the church.

My seminary years coincided with the release of Elisabeth Kubler-Ross's groundbreaking *On Death & Dying*, a book growing out of her work with dying patients and their families. From her clinical work, Kubler-Ross identified five stages that people experience when they're told that death is near. The stages are denial and isolation ("No, this can't be happening!"), anger ("This is the doctor's fault!"), bargaining ("God, if you give me a few more years, I'll serve you better"), depression ("I'm going to lose everyone and everything dear to me"), and finally acceptance. "Acceptance should not be mistaken for a happy stage," Kubler-Ross writes. "It is almost void of feelings. It is as if pain had gone, the struggle is over, and there comes a time for 'the final rest before the journey,' as one patient put it."[64] After many years in pastoral ministry, I've found that the stages aren't nearly as clear-cut as Kubler-Ross outlines. Some people skip stages altogether or experience them in a different order. But it is certainly true that coming to "see death as a friend," as Cardinal Bernardin puts it, and as an opportunity to make one last offering to Jesus, is a goal toward which we rightly strive. Acceptance for the Christian is no mere passive submission. It is a positive yielding of ourselves, at the hour of our death, into the care of the Lord of Life.

More than that, Paul says, "the time of my departure has come." The Greek word here for time, *kairos*, means more than the hours that happen to appear on a clock. The New Testament often uses *kairos* to refer to a critical moment, a turning point. "The time is fulfilled, and the kingdom of God has come near; repent, and believe in the good news" (Mark 1:15). The inaugural word of Jesus' ministry was a *kairos* moment, a radical shift at the dawn of a new age. Paul's death is his own *kairos*, as much a part of God's plan as his dramatic conversion or his itinerant ministry. His "departure," as well, is deeply grounded in Jesus' redeeming work. The Greek word stems from the root *luo*, which can refer to setting a prisoner free or unhooking animals from the cart they have been pulling. Just as Paul was set free from sin through the blood of Jesus, so now he will soon be set free from the burdens of apostolic ministry: set free in order to share in "an eternal weight of glory beyond all measure" (2 Corinthians 4:17).

Paul is no longer ambivalent about death. Years before, writing to his friends in Philippi, he was less certain. "For to me, living is Christ and dying is gain. If I am to live in the flesh, that means fruitful labor for me; and I do not know which I prefer." In the midst of his labors, it didn't seem the right moment to lay down his work. "I am hard pressed between the two: my desire is to depart and be with Christ, for that is far better; but to remain in the flesh is more necessary for you" (Philippians 1:21-24). But the time of ambivalence is past. He could pray, with Simeon, "Master, now you are dismissing your servant in peace, according to your word; for my eyes have seen your salvation, which you have prepared in the presence of all peoples" (Luke 2:29-31). Paul has come to accept his impending death. Perhaps Dietrich Bonhoeffer's words capture Paul's heart. Like Paul, Bonhoeffer ended his life in prison, and like Paul, he pondered his experience as he awaited his execution. In 1944, in Tegel Prison in Berlin, he wrote "Stations on the Road to Freedom," a prose poem that highlights four spiritual elements that lead to freedom—Discipline, Action, Suffering, and Death. Bonhoeffer concludes:

> Come now, highest moment on the road to freedom eternal,
> Death, put down the ponderous chains and demolish the walls
> of our mortal bodies, the walls of our blinded souls, that we
> might finally see what mortals kept us from seeing. Freedom,

how long have we sought you through discipline, action, and suffering. Dying, we now behold your face in the countenance of God.[65]

For many years, my episcopal wanderings regularly took me on a drive down Indiana State Road 19 between Elkhart and Nappanee, a region of corn, soybeans, and small family farms. It is also a region with a strong Anabaptist presence—Mennonites, Amish, and Church of the Brethren in particular. One Anabaptist farmer has painted an enormous, billboard-sized sign on the side of his barn. It reads:

LIFE IS SHORT

DEATH IS SURE

SIN THE CAUSE

CHRIST THE CURE

While I would probably not emblazon my own house with such signage—it cries out for explanation, each phrase a sermon on its own—I found it spiritually helpful, every time I drove down State Road 19, to ponder the reality of death; helpful, yes, if somewhat troubling and even frightening. Death is indeed sure. Paul knew it, with some specificity. So, in the end, do we. Unlike Paul, most of us do not know in advance the specific hour of our death, but death will claim us all. The good news, of course, is that Jesus claims us as well, and his claim is eternal.

Now that Paul has faced the reality of the present moment, he turns his attention to the past. "I have fought the good fight, I have finished the race, I have kept the faith." He piles one picture on top of another to make a single point: Looking back across the decades, he has accomplished what Jesus asked him to do, though the accomplishment has come through struggle.

Paul's ministry, from start to finish, has been a "good fight." This is not a new concept. Earlier, Paul urged Timothy: "Fight the good fight of the faith" (1 Timothy 6:12). Twice he describes Christians strapping on a suit of armor and preparing for spiritual battle (Ephesians 6:10-17; 1 Thessalonians 5:8). Whether the battle is waged against demonic forces—"the cosmic powers of this present darkness" (Ephesians 6:12)—or against opponents of his apostolic ministry (2 Corinthians 13:1-3), conflict has followed Paul from the moment he began preaching in Damascus after his conversion (Acts 9:23-35). Hymns such as *Fight the Good Fight With All Thy Might* and *Onward Christian Soldiers* may have gone out of fashion, but the underlying reality remains the same in our day as in Paul's. Christians, lay persons and clergy alike, are engaged in a spiritual battle. Following Jesus is never easy. Nor is there any guarantee, in this life, that we will win the fight. Christians, then and now, die for their faith—or simply die in the faith. Christians, then and now, can be overwhelmed by discouragement. Christians, then and now, come to the end of their lives without visible signs of "success." What Jesus asks of Paul, and asks of us as well, is to fight the fight, however it comes out. The abbot of Gethsemani Abbey during Thomas Merton's first years as a monk had a motto: *"Tout pour Jesus, par Marie, toujours avec un sourire"*—"All for Jesus, through Mary, always with a smile."[66] The "good fight" may be utterly undramatic, like the seventeenth-century monk Brother Lawrence and his endless stack of dishes.[67] Whatever it is, fight the fight. Then smile and leave the results in God's hands.

Paul is in equally familiar territory when he talks about the "race." He has already reminded Timothy that "in the case of an athlete, no one is crowned without competing according to the rules" (2:5); and, many years before, he asked his friends in Corinth, "Do you not know that in a race the runners all compete, but only one receives the prize? Run in such a way that you may win it" (1 Corinthians 9:24). In these final words, however, Paul isn't so much concerned about winning the race as he is about simply arriving at the finish line. In the next sentence, he will refer to a heavenly crown, the prize at the end of the race. But first, in this triad of word pictures, the emphasis is on faithfulness, doing the thing that Jesus asks—however large or small—and getting the job done. While Paul doesn't define the race, what he's describing looks more like a marathon than a sprint. Apostolic ministry is a long slog, not a quick dash, and Paul has faithfully plodded on, mile after grueling mile.

And then, as he looks back at his life, Paul can say, "I have kept the faith." These are ambiguous words. He may mean, "I have been careful in seeing to it that the Christian community remains doctrinally pure." In 1:14, he commends the "good treasure," the body of doctrine that Christian leaders must teach and all Christians must embrace. "Contend for the faith that was once for all entrusted to the saints" (Jude 3), as a later New Testament writer commands. Our understanding of that faith and its essentials has grown and deepened in two thousand years, but we too plant ourselves on the bedrock of the faith so wonderfully passed on from generation to generation. "What Christians believe about Christ," as *The Book of Common Prayer* reminds us, "is found in the Scriptures and summed up in the creeds."[68] And so, we might conclude, Paul here is reflecting on his adherence to the faith that had been revealed to him on the road to Damascus and that he had taught in church after church as he traveled the roads and seaways of the Roman Empire.

On the other hand, "I have kept the faith" may point to Paul's faithfulness in following Jesus, his willingness to embrace an itinerant ministry, preaching the gospel and suffering on the gospel's behalf. Some interpreters believe that, in this introspective moment, Paul is offering a word of gratitude for the gift of an apostolic calling and the grace that God had given him to fulfill his commission (see Romans 1:5). Which is it, then? Maintaining the faith or being faithful to his calling? Perhaps both. He is, after all, speaking in broad terms, and as he dictates these last sentences, he may be mentally filling in the details but not spelling them out on paper. In any case, Paul comforts himself that he has done what Jesus asked him to do. We might well pray for that same gift.

Now that Paul has pondered the present moment and reflected on his past, he turns his attention to the future. "From now on there is reserved for me the crown of righteousness, which the Lord, the righteous judge, will give me on that day, and not only to me but also to all who have longed for his appearing." Paul does not doubt his eternal destiny. However grim his immediate fate and whatever he has endured through his long years of ministry, he knows where he is going. Elsewhere Paul affirms that his eternal future is more real, more solid, than the passing present. "We have a building from God, a house not made with hands, eternal in the heavens" (2 Corinthians 5:1). More than that, what comes next is no mere "survival" but rather sharing in the resurrection of Jesus himself. "If the Spirit of him who raised Jesus from the dead dwells in you, he who raised Christ from the dead will give life to your mortal bodies also through his Spirit that dwells in you" (Romans 8:11). We begin to experience eternal life now, as we are united with Jesus in baptism (Romans 6:3-5); and thus we can look into the future and say with confidence the words of the Nicene Creed, "We look for the resurrection of the dead, and the life of the world to come."[69] Not only does Paul know where he is going: So do we.

But what is the "crown of righteousness"? Most interpreters understand the phrase to refer to the wreath placed on the head of victors in athletic contests. When we finish the race, Jesus does indeed crown us, though unlike the Olympic wreath, it is "the crown of glory...that never fades away" (1 Peter 5:4). Paul is telling us, in effect, that what he did on Christ's behalf—what we do on Christ's behalf—does not go unnoticed—far from it. We are saved by grace through faith, but "created in Christ Jesus for good works" (Ephesians 2:10), and somehow our faithfulness is acknowledged or rewarded. As I write these words, I realize that I have no idea what I'm talking about. The "life of the world to come" is wondrously glorious, for we will gaze into the face of Jesus (1 John 3:2) in a renewed creation (Romans 8:19-23). Yet it is beyond our imagining. We do know, however, that the crown is not for Paul alone; it is for "all who have longed for [Christ's] appearing." The word translated "longed for" is *agapao*, the same word that we find in John 3:16 ("For God so loved the world"), Romans 5:8 ("God proves his love for us in that while we still were sinners Christ died for us"), and 1 John 4:7 ("Beloved, let us love one another"). The Revised Standard Version translates the phrase, "loved his appearing," which may better capture what Paul is getting at: The crown is for those who love Jesus, "myriads of myriads" (Revelation 5:11), a vast and numberless throng. Paul's eternal destiny, and ours, is communal. Just as our call to belong to Jesus and our call to belong to the church are inseparable, so we will receive the "crown of righteousness" together.

Paul's present/past/future reflection came to life for me a few years ago when I stumbled, quite accidentally, onto a worn and bedraggled Bible. It's not uncommon that church offices become the repository of religious cast-offs. People often take unappreciated statues, paintings, icons, books, and Bibles to the church in the hope that the items will find a suitable home. What happens, in reality, is that the items pile up in closets and corners and on bookshelves, an enormous and untidy jumble. The bishop's office is no exception. One day, overwhelmed by the mess, I decided that it was time to do a thorough cleaning, to throw out what in conscience we could consign to the garbage and to re-gift other items to parishes that might find a use for them. As we sorted through the piles, my eyes rested on an old, worn-out King James Version Bible. The cover, though leather, was scratched and marked. The pages, brittle to the touch, made a crinkling noise when they were turned. While the Bible had no publication date, the typestyle seemed to indicate that it came from the 1920s or 1930s, or perhaps earlier. It had sat around the bishop's office, unnoticed, for a long time.

What struck me most forcefully were the annotations. The Bible contained no indication of ownership—no bookplate, signature, or identifying mark. But the owner had clearly taken to heart the prayer book's admonition that we "read, mark, learn, and inwardly digest"[70] the scriptures. Every page included underlined passages. No chapter was left unmarked, not even the most obscure corners of Leviticus or 1 Chronicles. Every page also included marginal notes in an old-fashioned, feminine hand that I associate with digitized nineteenth-century letters. Some of the notes commented on the passage. Others posed questions. Still others made reference to parallel biblical citations. The very brittleness of the pages stemmed, in large part, from the thorough way that the Bible had been annotated by what seemed to be a fountain pen. (Or, I wondered, was it a pen that had to be dipped in an inkwell every few words?) At the back of the Bible, Sister Anonymous—that's how I found myself referring to her—kept a long, detailed prayer list, mostly names, with an indication of the need: healing, guidance, peace. Since the Bible had several blank pages at the end and before the maps, the prayer list was extensive indeed. Sometimes she put a check mark in front of someone's name, perhaps indicating that her prayer had been answered.

Sister Anonymous will always, this side of eternity, remain a mystery to me. I will never know her identity, her circumstances, the pressures she faced in her daily life, or the struggles she dealt with as she followed Jesus. But as I thumbed through her Bible, I knew myself to be in the presence of a holy woman. She had "fought the good fight...finished the race...kept the faith." I found myself yearning to be faithful as she was faithful. In the years since I stumbled across her Bible, I have returned repeatedly to those three verses in Paul's second letter to Timothy, and to this anonymous Christian who lived them with such devotion. These verses are well worth memorizing: Emblazoned on our hearts, they challenge us, encourage us, and give us hope.

QUESTIONS FOR REFLECTION

1. The Great Litany asks God to deliver us "from dying suddenly and unprepared." What does it mean to prepare for death? How can we do so without being morbid on the one hand or denying the reality of death on the other?

2. Looking back on his life, Paul reflected on fighting the good fight, finishing the race, keeping the faith. What images or word pictures describe your journey in ministry?

3. As you look back on your own life, where do you see spiritual victories to celebrate? Defeats to recognize? What effect do these victories or defeats have on your ongoing ministry?

4. What is the connection between the promise of a "crown of righteousness" and your life as a Christian today? How does that promise inspire you?

CHAPTER TWELVE

People Mourned and Celebrated

Do your best to come to me soon, for Demas, in love with this present world, has deserted me and gone to Thessalonica; Crescens has gone to Galatia, Titus to Dalmatia. Only Luke is with me. Get Mark and bring him with you, for he is useful in my ministry. I have sent Tychicus to Ephesus. When you come, bring the cloak that I left with Carpus at Troas, also the books, and above all the parchments. Alexander the coppersmith did me great harm; the Lord will pay him back for his deeds. You also must beware of him, for he strongly opposed our message.

At my first defense no one came to my support, but all deserted me. May it not be counted against them! But the Lord stood by me and gave me strength, so that through me the message might be fully proclaimed and all the Gentiles might hear it. So I was rescued from the lion's mouth. The Lord will rescue me from every evil attack and save me for his heavenly kingdom. To him be the glory forever and ever. Amen. Greet Prisca and Aquila, and the household of Onesiphorus. Erastus remained in Corinth; Trophimus I left ill in Miletus. Do your best to come before winter. Eubulus sends greetings to you, as do Pudens and Linus and Claudia and all the brothers and sisters. The Lord be with your spirit. Grace be with you.

—2 Timothy 4:9-22

I recently joined a Facebook group called "We are from Norwalk CT," which caters to people who make Norwalk their home or who grew up there. I fall into the latter category: From 1954-1962, my family lived in Rowayton, a section in southwestern Norwalk that faces Long Island Sound. A few weeks before the writing of this chapter, the following question appeared on the group's news feed: "Who was your favorite and most influential teacher in the Norwalk Public Schools?" I found my mind drifting back across the decades. Faces appeared unbidden in my memory: Mrs. Seifert, my sixth-grade teacher and the first to break through my painfully shy exterior; Mr. Bissell, the high school biology teacher who took me to task for poor study habits and whose criticism led me to rethink my life; Mr. Callahan, the history teacher who spent hours one-on-one debating philosophy with me.

As I pondered the teachers who had influenced my life, other faces also presented themselves to my mind: Rick, my first Christian friend, profoundly influential in my college-age conversion; university and seminary professors who challenged me and expanded my vision—Dr. Reaves, Dr. Larue, Father Crum, Father (later Bishop) Borsch, Dr. Casserley, Dr. Buttrick; priests who mentored me—Ralph, John, Paul, Marshall, Kim; bishops under whom I'd served—Frank Burrill, James Montgomery, Francis Eric Bloy, Robert Rusack, Victor Rivera, John-David Schofield; episcopal colleagues too many to list who showed me the ropes when, to my surprise, I stumbled into the episcopate (though I must mention one, Russ Jacobus of the Diocese of Fond du Lac, who was my officially appointed mentor; he listened patiently and advised sparingly but always appropriately); bishop predecessors in Northern Indiana, who offered their wisdom and experience without reservation—William C. R. Sheridan and Frank Gray; clergy with whom I've served on staff—Rob, Scot, Richard, Henry, David, SuzeAnne; lay leaders who modeled Christian faithfulness and whose love for Jesus has strengthened my faith—Connie, Jan, Marta, Bruce (who later became a priest and still later a bishop and who, to my sorrow, died just days after these words were written), Nick, Pat, Bob, Jerry, Susie, Debby, John, Pat, Perry, Kitty, Tim, Sharon, Charlotte, Marie, Jon, and a numberless host of brothers and sisters in the parishes and the diocese I have been privileged to serve. As you skim this long list, the names are just that: names. But as I read the list, I see the faces of beloved friends who have shaped and formed my life and helped me to be the Christian I am today.

Yet honesty requires that I mention another list, at least by title. Not all relationships have a happy ending, and not every face that presents itself to my mind brings joy. Some teachers were bullies. Some colleagues were jealous, self-serving, or rude. Some lay leaders were hypercritical and negative. In the brokenness of human nature, we fail one another, and, I imagine, there are people who justly include me on their negative list. I beg their forgiveness and their prayers.

Paul ends his second letter to Timothy with just such a list of friends who have encouraged him and friends who have broken his heart. His letters typically conclude with personal greetings, and this one does as well—with a difference: Death approaches, and he allows his mind to range over the people who have touched his life. He remembers people who have served faithfully, people he yearns to see once more, and, yes, people who have let him down, abandoned him, or betrayed him. He is lonely. "Do your best to come to me soon," he begins, and the words sound plaintive. Indeed, he will intensify them a few sentences later. "Do your best to come before winter," Paul says, a reference to the fact that if Timothy doesn't make the sea voyage to Italy before storms begin in November, he will have to postpone the trip for many months. In these closing paragraphs, Paul will mention a few people who are nearby, but mostly he is alone, his empty hours devoid of people. And so, in his mind's eye, he sees faces, recalls the spiritual battles they have fought together, and grieves the relationships that have ended painfully. He is doing the stock taking that is a natural part of confronting death, a clear-eyed look at the people he mourns and the people he celebrates. As he takes stock, Paul provides a model for Timothy and for us.

First, he mourns. "Demas, in love with this present world, has deserted me and gone to Thessalonica." Demas had once been a loyal co-worker of Paul (Colossians 4:14; Philemon 24), but something has happened. We don't know the circumstances of his desertion. Did Demas intentionally abandon Paul or simply drift away? Perhaps, like the "seed that fell among thorns," Demas allowed the "cares of the world, and the lure of wealth, and the desire for other things [to] come in and choke the word" (Mark 4:7, 19). Whatever the details, we know that Demas has left and Paul is bereft. But if Demas's departure has broken Paul's heart, another betrayal cuts even more deeply. "Alexander the coppersmith did me great harm." Again, details are lacking. Timothy may know the nature of Alexander's offense, but we do not. At this distance, Alexander's specific identity is not clear. In 1 Timothy, Paul mentions an Alexander "whom I have turned over to Satan" (1 Timothy 1:20). This may well be the same person, though some scholars speculate that the Alexander appearing in Acts 19:33—a Jew who inserted himself into the riot over statues of Artemis in Ephesus—may have followed Paul to Rome and caused trouble for the imprisoned apostle. Whoever Alexander may have been, Paul is convinced that "the Lord will pay him back for his deeds." This is not a prayer for retribution but a statement of fact: Actions have consequences. Paul feels threatened and betrayed by Alexander, and he cautions Timothy, "You also must beware of [Alexander], for he strongly opposed our message."

Several other names appear, though it is uncertain whether these brothers have abandoned Paul or, instead, are simply "on assignment" elsewhere. "Crescens has gone to Galatia, Titus to Dalmatia." We know nothing about Crescens; this is his only reference in the New Testament. Titus, on the other hand, receives frequent mention as a traveling companion of Paul. "As for Titus," Paul writes the Christians in Corinth, "he is my partner and co-worker in your service" (2 Corinthians 8:23), and of course, one of the other pastoral letters is addressed to him. Because there are no negative words describing either Crescens or Titus, it is probable that their absence is related to ministry elsewhere and not to anything nefarious or unfaithful. This is certainly the case with one other missing brother. "I have sent Tychicus to Ephesus," Paul says. Even though Crescens, Titus, and Tychicus are, in all likelihood, absent for completely honorable reasons, Paul remains lonely. The sum total is a painful reality. Two brothers have deserted him, three others are doing "kingdom work" far away, and meanwhile, Paul is alone, in prison, and awaiting death.

To underscore his loneliness, Paul writes, "At my first defense no one came to my support, but all deserted me." Once more, he doesn't supply the details. Timothy, the letter's recipient, probably knows them, and Paul does not need to spell out the particulars in writing. He seems to be referring to some sort of preliminary hearing. Where that fits in the long and tangled history of Paul's arrest, imprisonment in Caesarea, multi-stop journey to Rome, and now confinement in the capital of the Roman Empire, we do not know. What's important, and what grieves Paul, is his sense of abandonment. At the end of his ministry, with the forces of darkness closing in and death at the executioner's hand a certainty, he wrestles with profound disappointment. Many of those dearest to him have not chosen to support him to the end.

We shouldn't be surprised. Christians continue to disappoint one another, and many bear the scars of wounds inflicted in—and by—the church. Sometimes, as Paul experiences, brothers and sisters fail to respond when we face a crisis. At other times, perhaps more rarely, Christians are the victims of genuine malice within the community. More frequently, Christians are wounded unintentionally in the rough and tumble of church conflict. Years ago, for example, I found myself in sharp disagreement with a colleague whom I will call Harry. We were struggling over a matter of church policy, and at first our exchanges were cordial, even humorous, as we tried and failed to find common ground. Over time, however, each of us solidified our positions. We became increasingly implacable, and our emails took on a harsher tone. Back and forth it went, an adult version of a playground fight. "You're wrong!" "No, you're wrong!" Eventually, I'd had it. How could Harry be so blind? Why couldn't he listen to common sense? And so, late one night, I fired off a final email. I took Harry to task for his poor theology, his weak grasp of the church's polity, his refusal to be sensible. With great satisfaction I clicked the "send" button and went to bed confident that I'd finally bettered Harry.

And then, at 2 am, I realized what I had done. I snapped awake, sat up in bed, and gasped, "Oh no!" Over and over I had promised "to respect the dignity of every human being,"[71] and now I had failed to do so. Not only failed but failed spectacularly! I ran into my study, fired up my computer, and wrote a frenzied email begging Harry for his forgiveness. Harry responded graciously, but things have never been the same between us. Whenever we meet, there's an awkward feeling to our encounters. In this life, the breach may never be healed. My relationship with Harry will always have a precious yet bittersweet flavor. When we survey our lives, all of us, like Paul, see an intricate mixture of relationships: some broken, some strained, some (as it's often put today) complicated.

But in the face of that mixture, Paul also celebrates. He is aware of a community of friends—a few near, mostly far—who love him, support him, and hold him in prayer. Just one traveling companion remains close at hand. "Only Luke is with me." We know Luke as the author of the gospel that bears his name and of the Book of Acts, and many scholars believe that the famous "we" passages in Acts reflect Luke's own firsthand experience of Paul's apostolic journeys. Beginning at Acts 16:10, several sections of the book are written in the first-person plural and appear to be eyewitness accounts of some of the more dramatic events in Acts: Paul crossing into Europe, the conversion of the Philippian jailer, the final journey to Jerusalem, Paul's arrest in the temple, and the long voyage to Rome. Paul also mentions Luke in Colossians 4:14 (calling him "the beloved physician") and in Philemon 24; in both cases, Luke is paired, rather surprisingly, with Demas, who we see later deserts Paul. It is not clear why Luke alone can remain with Paul in Rome, while others have gone, but his presence is no small matter. In the Roman Empire, prisoners were required to provide for their own needs, and so it was essential that they have friends on the "outside" to bring food and other necessities.

At the end of his letters, Paul typically sends greetings, a reminder of the interconnectedness of the church, even in a day when long-distance travel was difficult, dangerous, and rare. Paul rejoices in a caring, if distant, community of friends, and as he closes this letter, he acknowledges them gratefully. "Greet Prisca and Aquila," he says. Paul met this husband and wife team in Corinth (Acts 18:1-4), where they shared both a profession (tent-making) and a passion for evangelism. "Greet...the household of Onesiphorus," Paul adds. Earlier in the letter (1:16) he commended the same household for their spiritual and material support. "Erastus remained in Corinth; Trophimus I left ill in Miletus." Erastus, a government official (Romans 16:23), had been a traveling companion of Paul (Acts 19:22), and Trophimus accompanied the apostle on his final journey to Jerusalem (Acts 20:4). As with many of the names in Paul's letters, we know little biographical detail about these early Christian leaders. But clearly Paul holds them in high esteem, and as he prepares for his death, he greets them from afar.

Although only one traveling companion, Luke, remains in Rome, Paul's support system includes Roman Christians whom he had met for the first time when he arrived in the city after his long, eventful, and storm-tossed journey (Acts 28:11-15). "Eubulus sends greetings to you, as do Pudens and Linus and Claudia and all the brothers and sisters." We know nothing about these Christians, with the exception of Linus. Irenaeus of Lyons, writing a century later in his treatise *Against Heresies*, notes that "[w]hen the blessed apostles had founded and built up the Church, they handed over the ministry of the episcopate to Linus. Paul mentions this Linus in his Epistles to Timothy."[72] The future second bishop of Rome is among those aiding Paul!

An apparently throwaway line points to a miraculous transformation and the healing of a broken relationship. "Get Mark and bring him with you, for he is useful in my ministry." Mark, a Jerusalem Christian sometimes called John, accompanied Paul and Barnabas on their first missionary journey (Acts 13:5). Early on, "John, however, left them and returned to Jerusalem" (Acts 13:13). We don't know the circumstances of his departure. Was he exhausted? Frightened? Or had he simply lost enthusiasm for the work? Whatever the reason, Barnabas later wanted to rehabilitate him. As Paul and Barnabas prepared for a second journey,

> Barnabas wanted to take with them John called Mark. But Paul decided not to take with them one who had deserted them in Pamphylia and had not accompanied them in the work. The disagreement became so sharp that they parted company; Barnabas took Mark with him and sailed away to Cyprus. But Paul chose Silas and set out, the believers commending him to the grace of the Lord (Acts 15:37-40).

All too often, broken relationships go unhealed in this life, but in the case of Paul and Mark, and Barnabas as well, something wonderful has happened. We don't know precisely what. As is so often the case, the scriptures leave much of the story untold. Did someone intervene and bring these leaders together for face-to-face conversation? Did Paul or Barnabas or Mark have a change of heart and seek a rapprochement? All that we know—not only from the reference in 2 Timothy, but also from Colossians 4:10 and

Philemon 24—is that Paul and Mark and Barnabas have reconciled and that Paul can now request Mark's presence in this darkest of hours. The Mark who once deserted Paul is now "useful" in his ministry. The healing of the relationship between Paul and his former traveling companions is a powerful sign that the "ministry of reconciliation" (2 Corinthians 5:18) is both vertical and horizontal: We are reconciled to God the Father through the life, death, and resurrection of Jesus Christ; and we are reconciled to one another because Jesus is our peace (Ephesians 2:14).

Paul makes two practical requests of Timothy. "When you come, bring the cloak that I left with Carpus at Troas, also the books, and above all the parchments." The cloak (Greek *phailones*) was a circular garment made out of heavy material, with a hole in the center for the head, like a modern-day poncho. Paul, as we see, urges Timothy to "come before winter," and the cloak will help him to ward off the chill. The books (probably papyrus rolls) and parchments (animal skins) are a source of ongoing conjecture. What is in Paul's library? What does he like to read? As something of a book voyeur—I'm constantly scanning people's bookshelves, wondering what they're reading and what I might want to borrow—I wish that I could do the same scan of Paul's books, but alas, we will never know the contents of Paul's library. Some scholars speculate that the library included the Hebrew Scriptures, or an early form of the material that made its way into the gospels, or perhaps Paul's legal documents such as his citizenship papers. Whatever the case, it's clear that Paul's books were an important part of his spiritual and intellectual life.

As he celebrates his friends, near and far, Paul is supremely aware of God's constant presence in his prison cell. "The Lord stood by me and gave me strength, so that through me the message might be fully proclaimed and all the Gentiles might hear it. So I was rescued from the lion's mouth. The Lord will rescue me from every evil attack and save me for his heavenly kingdom. To him be the glory for ever and ever. Amen." Although some have deserted him and others failed to stand by him at his preliminary hearing, he is strengthened to say what he needs to say. The "lion's mouth" is probably not a literal reference to the lion's den; that particularly cruel form of execution for Christians is still some years in the future. Rather, Paul is saying that he has been kept safe in this difficult moment, empowered to speak a gospel word to the Roman legal authorities, and is confident that he will forever be embraced in God's care. While his earthly end is near, an eternal destiny awaits him. Paul cherishes his friends and relies on God.

We will never know if Timothy manages to travel to Rome before Paul's execution. Paul hopes Timothy will come—and soon, and yet, at the same time, he senses the approach of death. These are indeed his "famous last words." And so he closes his letter with a double-barreled goodbye. "The Lord be with your spirit. Grace be with you." In the English language, the word "you" can be both singular and plural. The best that we can do in English, if we're trying to make a distinction, is some variation of "you" versus "y'all." In Greek, however, the pronoun "you" has a singular and a plural form, and Paul uses them both in these two sentences. "The Lord be with your spirit": this is singular, Paul's final blessing to his young apprentice. He has nurtured his protégé, taught him, opened his heart to him, and treated him as a son, and now he places Timothy in God's good care. "Grace be with you." Here, "you" is plural. It is as though Paul is intuitively aware that these final words to Timothy will not be for Timothy alone but for the generations of Christians who will read them and find challenge and encouragement in them. You and I are the beneficiaries of Paul's second letter to Timothy. The Apostle Paul is our mentor as surely as he was Timothy's.

QUESTIONS FOR REFLECTION

1. Who are the people who have made the deepest impact on your life as a Christian? How did they model discipleship, and what did they teach you about your own response to Jesus' call?

2. Paul mourns the colleagues who have abandoned or betrayed him. How have you dealt with the painful reality that fellow Christians sometimes fail you, intentionally or unintentionally—and the equally painful reality that you, in turn, have failed others?

3. Who are your encouragers—the people who support you, counsel you, and challenge you to follow Jesus faithfully? How does their encouragement touch your daily life?

4. At the end of his life, Paul reconciled with Barnabas and Mark. How have you experienced a healed relationship? Are there people in your life today with whom you need to seek reconciliation?

EPILOGUE

Unlikely Mentors

Feet. I always dread Maundy Thursday, the day when Christians remember the Last Supper. At the end of that final meal with his friends, Jesus "got up from the table, took off his outer robe, and tied a towel around himself. Then he poured water into a basin and began to wash the disciples' feet and to wipe them with the towel" (John 13:4-5). Peter, as always the first to speak, objects. "You will never wash my feet," he declares (13:8). But Jesus insists, Peter finally gives in, and Jesus explains the point of the foot washing: "So if I, your Lord and Teacher, have washed your feet," he tells the disciples, "you also ought to wash one another's feet" (13:14). And so, on the night when Christians reflect on the meal and its aftermath, many churches have adopted an additional ceremony, as a sign of the mutual service to which we're all called. We wash feet.

The foot washing itself can be done in a number of ways. In some churches, the priest or pastor simply recruits twelve volunteers and washes their feet, a visual reminder of Jesus kneeling down in front of his twelve disciples. In other churches, however, the foot washing is a more participatory event. At the Cathedral of St. James in South Bend, Indiana, for example, the entire congregation is invited to wash one another's feet. Anyone who wishes can serve as a foot washer and also have their own feet washed. I dread this liturgical act, in part because I'm sensitive about my feet, and in part because the whole business feels awkward—as it should. But one year, the Maundy Thursday foot washing became more than a sign. It became, for a brief moment, the real thing.

The liturgy began unremarkably enough, with an opening hymn, prayer, and scripture readings. At some point during the readings, a homeless man entered the church and sat somewhere in the middle of the congregation. This is nothing unusual at St. James'. The parish is located downtown, and quite often, homeless people find their way into the church building; it's a place of warmth, both literally and spiritually. From my presider's chair, I noticed the man and found myself worrying. What will happen when it's time to wash feet? Will he want his feet washed? How will people react? After the sermon, I gave the invitation for the foot washing. Those who wanted to take part made their way to the altar area, the homeless man among them. By accident of placement, just behind him was a little girl, perhaps seven or eight years old, which meant that she would be the one to wash the man's feet. He sat in the designated chair and removed his shoes and socks, and it was obvious even from a distance that his feet needed to be washed. The foot washing would not be merely symbolic. The little girl knelt before him, her mother beside her, and the congregation held its breath. She reached into the bucket of warm water for soap and washcloth and, with great tenderness, washed the homeless man's feet.

Mentors come in all shapes, sizes, colors, and ages. Sometimes, of course, our mentors are easily identified. They may be teachers, employers, pastors, or older and more experienced Christian friends. But at other times, mentorship happens spontaneously and by surprise. Someone enters our lives, perhaps only briefly, and we are enriched, encouraged, and challenged to follow Jesus more faithfully. In other words, the mentors who shape our lives represent not a narrow subset of teachers but a wider and often surprising group of friends and, yes, of strangers. And so, that Maundy Thursday, a little girl showed a community of Christians what servanthood looks like. No words were necessary. The traditional definition of sacraments as outward and visible signs of inward and spiritual grace[73] seems especially apt. We saw grace in action that night, a sacramental encounter, and the memory of the little girl kneeling before the homeless man is seared into my heart forever. She became, in a grace-filled moment, mentor to a room full of adult Christians. Sometimes mentorship works that way. We learn from those who are younger and seemingly less experienced.

Jesus himself set the stage for that sacramental moment on Maundy Thursday. The disciples once asked him, "Who is the greatest in the kingdom of heaven?" He pointed to a child and said, "Truly I tell you, unless you change and become like children, you will never enter the kingdom of heaven. Whoever becomes humble like this child is the greatest in the kingdom of heaven" (Matthew 18:1-4). Leaders do well, Jesus is telling his friends, to cultivate in themselves the childlike qualities of wonder, spontaneity, simplicity, and humility. In other words, look for unlikely and surprising mentors.

The apostle Paul himself is just such an unlikely and surprising mentor. By his own account, he presented a less than impressive appearance. "His letters are strong," he notes that some complained, "but his bodily presence is weak, and his speech contemptible" (2 Corinthians 10:10). He suffered from an unnamed and unpleasant illness as well. "You know that it was because of a physical infirmity that I first announced the gospel to you," he reminds the Christians in Galatia; "though my condition put you to the test, you did not scorn or despise me" (Galatians 4:13-14). While the New Testament contains no physical description of Paul, the second century "Acts of Paul" says that he was "a man of middling size, and his hair was scanty, and his legs were a little crooked, and his knees were far apart; he had large eyes, and his eyebrows met, and his nose was somewhat long."[74] His personality has what today we call rough edges. In a fit of anger, for example, he denounces the Christians in Galatia as foolish and even suggests that proponents of circumcision mutilate themselves (Galatians 3:1; 5:12). But I'm not implying that we are somehow wrong in naming Paul a saint and including his writings in the canon of scripture. Far from it! Paul demonstrates a principle found in the Bible from Genesis to Revelation: that God uses unsuitable people to accomplish God's purposes. From Noah to Abraham, from Moses to David, and from Peter to Paul, unlikely people become leaders, mentors, and exemplars of heroic faith. They teach us not despite who they are, but because of who they are.

Ted told me the story of his conversion to Christianity, a conversion as unlikely as it was dramatic. He had been raised in a Christian church, but as is so often the case, his Christian upbringing hadn't "taken." In his teen years, he drifted away and entered a time of exploration. At first, he worshiped in other Christian faith traditions. He drifted from the Roman Catholic Church to an evangelical megachurch to an Eastern Orthodox parish whose icon-rich walls appealed to him and frightened him. But in the end, nothing satisfied him; nothing fed the deep hunger that he felt for a connection with God. It wasn't that these churches did anything wrong, he told me. The problem was in him. He simply couldn't bring himself to say an unqualified yes to the Lord. And so his explorations became more esoteric. He plunged briefly into Buddhism and Hinduism, then into various forms of New Age spirituality. On one occasion, he said, he even visited a witches' coven. The experience at once fascinated and appalled him. Finally, in desperation, Ted remembered that he'd seen a house in his town with a sign that advertised "Psychic Reader." He thought, "Why not?" He made an appointment, paid his fee, and poured out his story to the psychic. She was, he said, bizarrely dressed in a voluminous robe and some kind of turban. Her office was decorated with a pastiche of religious symbols, from the cross of Christianity to the star of David of Judaism to the crescent of Islam; from New Age moons and stars to various shapes, sizes, and colors of crystals. There was even, he said, a crystal ball, straight from Professor Marvel's wagon in *The Wizard of Oz*. The psychic listened to Ted's story, sat silently for a while, then looked up at him through rheumy eyes, and said, "You need more Jesus." Those were her exact words, Ted told me. "You need more Jesus," she repeated, and fell into some kind of swoon. Ted stood up, ran from the psychic's office, jumped into his car, and drove down the street. By chance, he noticed the sign for a church (it happened to be an Episcopal church, thus our connection) and made a mental note. The next Sunday, he worshiped there, and the next, and the next. He was finally ready to say yes, and he told me his story on the day that I confirmed him. An unlikely mentor? More than unlikely: utterly unsuitable, doubtless a charlatan, not even a Christian. Her flaws were as blatant as the turban on her head. And yet, by God's grace, she was an essential turning point in Ted's journey to Jesus Christ.

By contrast, Paul as mentor seems almost conventional! When Paul writes his "famous last words," to be sure, Timothy is well aware of his mentor's flaws. After all, he has spent years with Paul and has seen him in action and close at hand. While we have no biblical record of how Timothy reacts to Paul's sometimes-prickly personality, we can imagine that he has moments when he throws up his hands. "Paul, get a grip," he might say in frustration. "Can't you lighten up?" It could be that Paul learns some things from his young apprentice. Mentorship can go both ways. Regardless, Paul, apostle and mentor, friend and companion, forms Timothy's life and prepares him for his own apostolic work. It is precisely through Paul, and not some spiritual superhero, that Timothy becomes the leader who guides the church in its post-apostolic era.

Paul's example reminds us that we should not expect to find mentors who have gotten it all together! Mentors and protégés alike are flawed and sinful people. "All have sinned and fall short of the glory of God," Paul himself says (Romans 3:23), and he makes it clear that he joins in humanity's rebellion against God: "I do not understand my own actions. For I do not do what I want, but I do the very thing I hate" (Romans 7:15). Nor should we look for Christian mentors whose spiritual maturity far exceeds our maturity. Mentors struggle as we struggle, ask the questions that we ask, wrestle with doubts as debilitating as our own. They are fellow pilgrims. Whether we are in a formal mentor-and-apprentice relationship or experience mentorship "on the run," our mentors share a journey with us—a journey in which we yield ourselves, often slowly and agonizingly, to Jesus, who bids us to take up our cross and follow him.

Soon after he receives this final letter from Paul, Timothy inherits the burden of apostolic leadership. Paul has tutored, taught, and mentored him, and the memory of this long and fruitful relationship sustains Timothy in the decades that follow. So it is for us! We, like Timothy, are the recipients of wondrous grace. God has used our mentors to teach us, challenge us, and demonstrate for us the joy and the cost of Christian discipleship. By his grace, God has used us as well to mentor others. I invite you to join me in giving thanks for the mentors who have touched your life. They, and we, are unlikely Christians. They, and we, are unlikely leaders. That is always God's way. Our mentors, even the most surprising, have shown us the heart of Jesus. We are stronger and more faithful Christians because of their faithful ministry. May we, with equal faithfulness, make Jesus known to all whom God puts in our path.

A Word of Thanks

This book had its origin in an invitation from the Rt. Rev. Sean Rowe, bishop of Northwestern Pennsylvania and Western New York, to offer a retreat for the clergy. As I cast about for possible topics, my mind leapt to Paul's second letter to Timothy, pastoral advice par excellence and a superb example of apostolic mentorship. Later, I delivered versions of the same retreat to the clergy of the Diocese of Albany, the Diocese of South Dakota, and my own Diocese of Northern Indiana. While not formally in retreat format, I "test marketed" some of this material to groups of lay leaders. I am profoundly grateful to all of these leaders, clergy and lay, for their warm reception, their feedback, and their suggestions. The Diocese of Northern Indiana kindly gave me a transitional sabbatical as my active ministry drew to a close, and during those months, I began the long process of turning sketchy notes on a yellow pad into readable prose. After my retirement, the reading room of the Theodore M. Hesburgh Library on the campus of the University of Notre Dame became my preferred writing place, thanks to the gracious gift of a parking pass from the university. I can hardly imagine a more fitting setting to ponder, pray, and write!

I could not have written this book alone. Friends and family urged me to complete the task and helped me to carve out blocks of time to read, ponder, and write. My community of support is too large and varied to attempt to list, though I must make one exception. The Rev. Susan B. Haynes (now bishop of Southern Virginia) and the people of St. Paul's Episcopal Church, Mishawaka, Indiana, have encouraged me in countless ways, and I am grateful beyond words for their love and care for my wife and me.

I am deeply grateful as well to the Rev. Scott Gunn, Richelle Thompson, and the staff of Forward Movement as well as the Rev. Nancy Hopkins-Greene for their support, suggestions, and superb expertise. Shepherding a book from raw manuscript to publication requires a team of dedicated professionals, and it has been a gift to work with them and to be the beneficiary of their encouragement.

Writing a book on mentoring inevitably led me to recall the hundreds of people who have prayed for me, enriched my life, and challenged me to follow Jesus more faithfully. They are lay and clergy, young and old, famous and obscure. Some are writers whom I have never met but whose writing stretched my faith; others are figures from the distant Christian past. Parishioners in the four parishes I served and in the diocese I was privileged to lead provided a kind of training course in Christian leadership. They taught me how to lead, courageously pointed out my failures, and showed me the "more excellent way" (1 Corinthians 12:31) that builds up the body of Christ. Many of those mentors make their appearance in these pages; others, some long dead, live only in my heart. Perhaps the greatest blessing that has come to me in writing *The Heart of a Leader* is the opportunity to remember with profound gratitude the people who have shaped my life. Paul's words are especially apt. "I have received much joy and encouragement from your love, because the hearts of the saints have been refreshed through you" (Philemon 7). My mentors, too, have brought me joy, encouraged me, refreshed me—and I offer this book as a thank you note to them.

Endnotes

[1] Benedict of Nursia, *The Rule of St. Benedict*, trans. Leonard J. Doyle (Collegeville: Liturgical Press, 1948), p. 5

[2] Benedict, 73

[3] Benedict, 1

[4] Augustine of Hippo, *Confessions*, trans. R. S. Pine-Coffin (Middlesex: Penguin Books, 1961), 69-70

[5] Augustine, 178-9

[6] The term "baptism in the Holy Spirit" is imprecise and perhaps might better be defined as praying for ongoing renewing work of the Spirit given to us in our baptism. Baptism is described in *The Book of Common Prayer* (p. 298) as "full initiation by water and the Holy Spirit into Christ's Body the Church."

[7] C. S. Lewis, *Letters to Malcolm: Chiefly on Prayer* (London: Collins, 1966), 47

[8] *The Book of Common Prayer*, (New York: Church Publishing Incorporated, 1979), 308

[9] *The Hymnal 1982* (New York: Church Publishing Incorporated, 1985), 576

[10] Mark Galli and Ted Olsen, eds., *131 Christians Everyone Should Know* (Nashville: Broadman & Holman Publishers, 2000), 377

[11] It is worth noting that later generations of Christians have come to repudiate these tragic Reformation-era killings. At the Church of St. Mary the Virgin in Oxford, for example, a plaque reads: "Remember the martyrs of the Reformation, both Catholic and Protestant, who lived in Oxfordshire, taught at the University of Oxford, or were brought here for execution." The plaque lists the names of both Protestant and Catholic martyrs, theological antagonists who died for their understanding of the faith.

[12] Dietrich Bonhoeffer, *The Cost of Discipleship* (New York: Touchstone, 1995), 87

[13] Joshua Piven and David Borgenicht, *The Worst-Case Scenario Survival Handbook* (San Francisco: Chronicle Books, 1999), 14

[14] Benedict, 80

[15] It is not entirely clear if Titus has abandoned Paul, or if he has simply gone away on a ministry trip and left Paul behind.

[16] Sermon excerpts taken from David Hyndman's unpublished manuscript and used by permission.

[17] *The Book of Common Prayer*, 855

[18] Joseph Ratzinger, *Co-Workers of the Truth: Meditations for Every Day of the Year* (San Francisco: Ignatius Press, 1992), 224

[19] Events sometimes have surprising consequences. The priest who eventually did accept the call as assistant professor of pastoral theology at Trinity, the Rev. Laurie Thompson, has had a long and fruitful ministry there and now serves as the seminary's dean. At the same time, I've come to believe that at least part of God's intention in keeping me at All Saints was to prepare me for my ministry as Bishop of Northern Indiana. But none of this was obvious when I hit that "wall" on the jet bridge!

[20] *The Book of Common Prayer* [1928] (Greenwich: Seabury Press, 1928), 555

[21] C. S. Lewis, *The Screwtape Letters* (New York: The Macmillan Company, 1961), 115-6

[22] George A. Buttrick, *Sermons Preached in a University Church* (New York: Abingdon Press, 1959), 7

[23] I am sometimes told that I preach "like a Presbyterian." Whether this is a comment on content or sermon length, I take it as a compliment, for it recalls Dr. Buttrick to my heart and mind.

[24] *The Book of Common Prayer*, 864

[25] Marshall Broomhall ed., *The Chinese Empire: A General and Missionary Survey* (London: Morgan and Scott, 1907), 374

[26] Graham Turner, *God's People and the Seduction of Empire* (Durham: Sacristy Press, 2016), 168

[27] I will describe how this happened in Chapter Nine.

[28] *The Book of Common Prayer* [1928], 539-40; italics mine

[29] *The Book of Common Prayer*, 304-5

[30] Lewis, *Screwtape*, 75

³¹ I use the words progressive and conservative reluctantly and might well put them in quotation marks. Rarely are Christians entirely in one "camp" (another inexact word) or the other. But the point is clear: Whatever the perspective, conflict can quickly escalate as angry words fly back and forth.

³² Christian Smith and Melinda Lundquist Denton, *Soul Searching: The Religious and Spiritual Lives of American Teenagers* (New York: Oxford University Press, 2005), 162-3

³³ See Richard Bauckham, *Jesus and the Eyewitnesses: The Gospels As Eyewitness Testimony* (Grand Rapids: William B. Eerdmans Publishing Co., 2006), 8

³⁴ See the conclusion of Jack's story at the end of Chapter Three.

³⁵ *The Book of Common Prayer*, 359

³⁶ *The Book of Common Prayer*, 854

³⁷ Lewis, *Screwtape*, 12

³⁸ G. Kittel, G. W. Bromiley, & G. Friedrich eds., *Theological Dictionary of the New Testament* (Grand Rapids: William B. Eerdmans Publishing Co., 1984), Vol. 3, 171

³⁹ C. S. Lewis, *God in the Dock: Essays on Theology and Ethics*, Walter Hooper, ed. (Grand Rapids: William B. Eerdmans Publishing Company, 1970), 152-153

⁴⁰ Thomas G. West and Grace Starry West, *Texts on Socrates: Plato and Aristophanes* (Ithica and London: Cornell University Press, 1998), 92

⁴¹ http://bolsinger.blogs.com/weblog/good-disappointing-leadership/

⁴² *Lesser Feasts and Fasts* 2003 (New York: Church Publishing Incorporated, 2003), 427

⁴³ J. B. Phillips, *The New Testament in Modern English* (New York: The Macmillan Company, 1962), 519. A 1972 revision of the translation changed "little tin gods" to the less colorful "dictators."

⁴⁴ Martin Thornton, *Pastoral Theology: A Reorientation* (Eugene: Wipf & Stock, 1958), 11

⁴⁵ Rod Dreher, *The Benedict Option: A Strategy for Christians in a Post-Christian Nation* (New York: Sentinel, 2017), 2

⁴⁶ Bonhoeffer, 63; italics in the original

⁴⁷ *The Book of Common Prayer*, 853

⁴⁸ *The Book of Common Prayer*, 236

[49] Karl Barth, *The Word of God and the Word of Man* (New York: Harper & Brothers, 1957), 28

[50] C. S. Lewis, *The Last Battle* (Harmondsworth: Penguin Books Ltd., 1956), 165

[51] https://www.washingtonpost.com/local/on-faith-local/gerald-a-larue-religious-scholar-who-debunked-bible-stories-dies-at-98/2014/09/22/46829878-4299-11e4-b47c-f5889e061e5f_story.html?utm_term=.8280d914b14c

[52] C. S. Lewis, *Surprised by Joy: The Shape of My Early Life* (New York: Harcourt, Brace & World, 1955), 191

[53] Athanasius of Alexandria, *Athanasius: The Life of Antony and the Letter to Marcellinus*, trans. Robert C. Gregg (Mahwah, NJ: Paulist Press, 1980), 31

[54] John Wesley, *The Works of the Rev. John Wesley* Vol. I (London: Thomas Blansard, 1809), 280

[55] Andrew Klavan, *The Great Good Thing: A Secular Jew Comes to Faith in Christ* (Nashville: Thomas Nelson, 2016), 247-8

[56] C. S. Lewis, *The Weight of Glory and Other Addresses* (Grand Rapids: William B. Eerdmans Publishing Co., 1965), 14-15; italics in the original

[57] Lewis, *The Weight of Glory*, 15

[58] J. R. R. Tolkien, *The Lord of the Rings: The Fellowship of the Ring* (New York: Ballantine Books, 1965), 76

[59] Standing Commission on Evangelism of the General Convention of the Episcopal Church, *Go Listen and Tell: The Presentation of Jesus Christ* (Cincinnati: Forward Movement, 1991), 7

[60] *The Book of Common Prayer*, 855

[61] *The Book of Common Prayer*, 149

[62] http://www.nytimes.com/1996/08/31/us/cardinal-bernardin-says-he-has-inoperable-cancer.html

[63] Joseph Cardinal Bernardin, *The Gift of Peace: Personal Reflections* (Chicago: Loyola Press, 1997), x

[64] Elisabeth Kubler-Ross, *On Death & Dying: What the Dying Have to Teach Doctors, Nurses, Clergy & Their Own Families* (New York: Scribner, 1969), 110

[65] https://renovare.org/articles/the-road-to-freedom

[66] Thomas Merton, *The Sign of Jonas* (San Diego: Harcourt, Inc., 1953), 121

[67] Brother Lawrence of the Resurrection, *The Practice of the Presence of God* (Washington, DC: ICS Publications, 1994), xxxvii

[68] *The Book of Common Prayer*, 851

[69] *The Book of Common Prayer*, 359

[70] *The Book of Common Prayer*, 236; this prayer is discussed in more detail in Chapter Nine

[71] *The Book of Common Prayer*, 305

[72] Cyril C. Richardson, ed., *Early Christian Fathers* (New York: Touchstone, 1996), 372

[73] *The Book of Common Prayer*, 857

[74] https://www.christianitytoday.com/history/issues/issue-47/bald-blind-single.html

About the Author

Edward S. Little was Bishop of Northern Indiana from 2000-2016. Born in New York City and raised in New York and Connecticut, he attended the University of Southern California and Seabury-Western Theological Seminary and served parishes in the dioceses of Chicago, Los Angeles, and San Joaquin prior to his election to the episcopate. He is the author of *Ears to Hear: Recognizing and Responding to God's Call, Joy in Disguise: Meeting Jesus in the Dark Times*, and articles in *The Living Church* and *Christianity Today*. Ed and his wife, Sylvia, are the parents of two children and the grandparents of Lani and Taj.

About
Forward Movement

Forward Movement is committed to inspiring disciples and empowering evangelists. Our ministry is lived out by creating resources such as books, small-group studies, apps, and conferences.

Our daily devotional, *Forward Day by Day*, is also available in Spanish (Adelante *Día a Día*) and Braille, online, as a podcast, and as an app for smartphones or tablets. It is mailed to more than fifty countries, and we donate nearly 30,000 copies each quarter to prisons, hospitals, and nursing homes.

We actively seek partners across the church and look for ways to provide resources that inspire and challenge. A ministry of the Episcopal Church for more than eighty years, Forward Movement is a nonprofit organization funded by sales of resources and by gifts from generous donors.

To learn more about Forward Movement and our resources, visit ForwardMovement.org. We are delighted to be doing this work and invite your prayers and support.